WHY NOT STAY FOR BREAKFAST?

A comedy

GENE STONE
and
RAY COONEY

SAMUEL  FRENCH

LONDON

NEW YORK   TORONTO   SYDNEY   HOLLYWOOD

WHY NOT STAY FOR BREAKFAST?

The play was first performed at the Palace Theatre, Westcliff-on-Sea, July 1970, with the following cast:

George Clarke	Ray Cooney
Louise Hamilton	Liz Edmiston
Jimmy	Ralph Arliss

The play directed by Ray Cooney

WHY NOT STAY FOR BREAKFAST?

Presented by Ray Cooney Productions Ltd
at the Apollo Theatre, London, on the 12th December 1973, with the following cast of characters:

George Clarke	Derek Nimmo
Louise Hamilton	Katy Manning
Davey	Sam Sewell
Hippy Boy	Edward Duke
Hippy Girl	Susan Holdnerness

The play directed by Ray Cooney
Setting by Hutchinson Scott

The action takes place in George Clarke's flat, in a late Victorian house in Hampstead

ACT I	A late September evening
ACT II	
Scene 1	Late afternoon, ten days later
Scene 2	The following morning

Time – the present

ACT I

George Clarke's flat. 9 p.m. on a September evening

The flat is on the first floor of a large Victorian house in Hampstead. The set is a converted large room, with a lounge area, taking up about two-thirds of the stage, R, and a kitchen area L. There are two low steps running up and downstage between the two areas. In the R wall is a large bay-window giving a view of roof-tops. The front door is in the back wall and opens on to a dingy landing and staircase. A door up L to the bedroom is separated from the lounge area by a short wall running on the line of the steps. In the bedroom is visible George's bed. Above the sink in the L wall is a single window, with a view of house backs and a brick wall. In the centre of the steps is a low oak chest, leaving plenty of room to pass above and below it. The flat is obviously a bachelor flat, very unfeminine, but with the walls covered in bric-a-brac and "old-fashioned" pictures. The furniture is from all periods except modern, and the room is very cluttered with odd bits and pieces which George has bought in second-hand shops. The lounge is furnished with an armchair, a large desk, bookshelves on the back wall, a gramophone, and a console table carrying drinks. There is a large put-u-up type settee with small tables at either end of it. The telephone is on the table R of the settee. There is a small console table to one side of the front door. The kitchen has a refrigerator, cupboards and shelves, an oven (practical) and a sink unit (also practical). The cupboards provide work-tops, with the oven and sink in between. There is a small round table downstage with two upright chairs. (See set plan at end of book.) Light switches are beside the front door, on the wall downstage of the drinks table, and beside the bedroom, for the kitchen lights

As the CURTAIN *rises, George is in the kitchen cooking his supper. He is in his late thirties, very neat-looking and prim. He wears a white shirt and striped tie, with well-pressed dark trousers, and braces. At the moment he is also wearing an apron. The kitchen table is laid for one person and also contains bowls of ingredients, scales, and a cookery book. There are three pans on the stove, containing rice, "Suki Yaki" and something (indiscernible) burning. There is a kitchen timer on the work-top. The kitchen is lit, but the lounge is in darkness except for a little street light showing through the half-open curtains*

After a moment the timer rings. George refers to the cookery book, takes something from the table and puts it in the Suki Yaki pan. As he does so, the telephone starts to ring. He hesitates, looks at his watch, nods, then carries on cooking. After a moment he regulates the heaters, then goes towards the settee. He stops and comes back, unhurriedly, to the light switch L. *He then moves back and sits beside the telephone, changes his mind, rises and turns on the standard lamp. He resumes his seat, picks up the telephone, and speaks immediately*

George (*on the phone*) Hullo, Helen . . . Mm? Wish I wouldn't do what? . . . I always say, "Hullo Helen" . . . Who else would it be? . . . In that case I'd simply say, "I'm sorry I thought you were my sister. She always rings at nine o'clock." Actually, you're five minutes late . . . The doctor, of course . . . Was I? I was busy in the kitchen . . . Suki Yaki . . . Suki Yaki. It's Japanese . . . Of course it won't upset my tummy. You know I like to experiment . . . Just me . . . No, no just me. What were you seeing the doctor about this time? (*As soon as he asks the question he realizes he shouldn't and holds the receiver away from him for a few seconds. He then listens again*) In the kidneys, oh dear. (*He listens again for a moment. Commiserating*) Oh dear . . . Oh dear . . . oh dear . . . (*Helen is obviously nattering on so George takes this opportunity to lay the phone in the armchair and hurry through to the kitchen. He quickly lowers all the gases. He hurries back to the phone but stops. He quickly pours himself a small whisky and soda and then picks up the phone*) Oh dear.

From above comes the sound of a record player playing an up-to-date number very loudly. George reacts

(*On the phone*) What was that? . . . I can't quite hear. There's a most extraordinary noise going on. They really shouldn't allow these hippy types in the flats here. Sometimes goes on all night . . . I have but it's like conversing in a foreign language . . . It started off with two young men but there's enough up there now to start a small demonstration. Now what were you saying, my love? . . . The doctor's worried about your liver . . . Your kidneys, I mean . . .

From upstairs has come the sound of an argument between Davey and Louise. Although no actual words are heard, Louise's voice is predominant

(*On the phone*) Oh dear, that's nasty . . . A specialist? (*He reacts to the noise upstairs*) I'm sorry I didn't hear that. They're at it again upstairs—it sounds more like an argument . . . Mm? No, I don't think a specialist would do you any—why don't you go and stay with Mummy in Bournemouth.

There is a sudden very loud crash from upstairs

Oh, my God, they're coming through! Heaven only knows.

The door upstairs opens and closes loudly

Helen, I think you'd better ring me back later. I can't concentrate. There's a frightful row going on and I just can't concentrate.

There is a sudden urgent ringing at his door

(*Startled*) Oh! (*On the phone*) There's someone at the door. Hang on a second. (*He inadvertently replaces the receiver, realises and immediately starts to re-dial. Still holding the phone, he goes to the door as the ringing is repeated*) All right, all right, I'm coming. (*He opens the door*)

Louise enters. She is a north-country girl about seventeen and dressed in the uniform of the young female nonconformist—a simple, shift that ends above her knees, long hair down over her shoulders, a large bag with shoulder strap and bare feet in sandals. She has an air of almost arrogant self-confidence. She is also very pregnant

George stares at her in blank amazement. She "waddles" from the door, goes to the settee and lays back on it. George, still agog, comes down to look at her

(*On the phone*) Er—Helen . . . Yes, I'm all right . . . Someone from upstairs . . . No, not one of the young men.

Louise opens her eyes on hearing this last remark

(*On the phone*) Helen, will you ring back in a few minutes . . . No, I won't get involved.

George puts the phone down and looks at Louise

(*After a moment*) Are you all right?
Louise That's a silly question.
George (*trying to be polite*) Would you like a glass of water?
Louise Have you got a coke?
George No, I'm afraid not. Is there anything else I could get you?
Louise (*referring to George's drink on the table*) What's this?
George Whisky and soda.
Louise I'll have one of those.
George Oh. (*Indicating her condition*) Do you think you should?
Louise (*patting her tummy*) It'll put hair on his chest.

George starts to pour her drink

(*Sitting up*) Oh that bloody bugger upstairs.

George winces slightly at the swearing

George I—er—there was rather a lot of noise.
Louise That was Davey and me.
George Davey?
Louise One of the fellows upstairs.
George Oh.
Louise We were having a row.
George I thought you might be.
Louise Oh that bloody bugger . . .
George (*quickly*) Yes, I heard you the first time.
Louise I hope his record player got broken.
George Record—is that what that crash was?
Louise Yes. His record player getting tossed around.
George He didn't throw it at you?

Louise No fear. I threw it at him.
George Good Lord. (*He hands her the drink*) There you are.

Louise takes a sip. It is quite strong

Louise This'll set him going.
George Set who going?
Louise Him in there (*patting her tummy*) with his feet. Boom-boom!

George gives an embarrassed nod. Louise gets up with her drink and walks around looking at the lounge

This is the same layout as the boys' place upstairs.
George Is that so?
Louise I suppose the downstairs flat is the same as well.
George Er—I should imagine so, yes.
Louise (*pointing to the bedroom*) That's your other room through there is it?
George Er—yes—bedroom.
Louise It's all one bloody bedroom upstairs. Hey you've done this up differently though. Are you in the second-hand furniture business?
George (*surprised*) No.
Louise (*laughing*) It looks like the "Old Curiosity Shop". Did you get landed with this lot by the last tenant?
George No I like to collect the odd thing, that's all.
Louise You didn't fix it up like this on purpose?
George Yes!
Louise (*looking around*) Well. Bugger me gently!

She goes into the kitchen, leaving George looking after her irritably

(*Calling out*) Kitchen's not bad.
George Thank you very much.
Louise Hey, there's a pan burning on the stove.
George Burning. Out of the way! Out of the way! (*Rushing through*) Oh, my goodness.

During the ensuing dialogue, George tries to sort out the various pans. One of the concoctions has got burnt and he runs the saucepan under the tap

Louise What is it?
George Various things. The main course is Suki Yaki.
Louise Sooky who?
George Suki Yaki. It's Japanese.
Louise You kinky devil.
George I see nothing kinky about liking Japanese food.
Louise Cooking it yourself though.
George (*concentrating on his pans*) That's right.
Louise (*looking at the cookery book*) Were you making it from this?
George Yes.
Louise Bloody hell, and scales too. Do you always use scales when you're cooking?

George Yes.

Louise Scales. Cookery books. Little apron. Proper do-it-yourself kit, aren't you?

George (*on his dignity*) I'm sure you didn't come here to discuss my culinary peculiarities.

Louise (*sending him up*) Bloody hell.

George And perhaps you could moderate your language.

Louise (*laughing*) And what about your bloody language?

George (*politely*) It's rather late and I'm——

Louise It's only ten past nine.

George (*pressing on*) —I'm in the middle of preparing my dinner.

Louise Sooky Pooky!

George Sooky Pooki—er—Yaki!

Louise (*laughing*) I'm only sending you up. (*Simply*) How would you like to give me some money?

George I beg your pardon?

Louise I said, "How would you like to give me some money?"

George What do you mean, "Give it to you?"

Louise I would say "lend" but you won't get it back.

George You're not serious.

Louise Of course I am.

George You can't just walk into somebody's flat and say, "How would you like to give me some money".

Louise I can.

George Well, if that doesn't take the biscuit.

Louise It's not bad this stuff. I've only had whisky a couple of times before. Up the revolution! (*She drinks*)

George Up the revo——! (*quietly*)—lution!

Louise A couple of quid will do actually.

George Pardon?

Louise A couple of quid will do.

George You realize this is begging, do you?

Louise It's not begging.

George What do *you* call it then?

Louise Can't you understand? I'm offering you a chance to share something with me.

George (*worried*) Share something?

Louise An experience. A little exchange of feeling between two people.

George Exchange of feeling?

Louise Relationship. Communication.

George (*sarcastically*) I see.

Louise You don't understand.

George Yes, I do. It's all part of this modern way of carrying on, isn't it. The youth movement. Live now pay later. Let's make love not war. Let's not bother to work, let's knock on some chap's door and ask for a couple of pounds.

Louise You don't half talk a load of balls.

George Will you stop using that sort of language.

Louise You're very uptight, do you know that?

George I haven't the faintest idea what "uptight" means but I'm sure you're right. Now as you've finished your drink, and as you seem to have calmed down a little, I suggest you return to your husband.

Louise What husband?

George How many husbands have you got?

Louise Bugger all.

George Oh. Well in that case I suggest you—er—return to—er—the father of your child.

Louise It's a hell of a walk to Bradford.

George The gentleman upstairs isn't . . .

Louise I'll tell you what he is——!

George Apart from that.

Louise I've only known him a week. I met him and this other guy in a café in Leicester Square.

George A week?

Louise Have you got a fag?

George A. . . ? Yes. (*He indicates the box*)

Louise Is that a fag box?

George Not really. It's funny you should say that. It's an early Victorian crumpet warmer. (*Louise giggles*) It really is most ingenious; the little flap goes up there, and the hot water goes in *there*, and the heat sort of permeates beneath your crumpet and warms it. It's Sheffield plate, actually —you can see the copper coming through. It's rather pretty, isn't it?

Louise Very pretty—can I have a fag? You see, I'd just come down from Bradford. I'd got nowhere to stay so Davey said I could crash in with them. Well, it's been one bloomin' row after another, so I've split.

George Why did you leave your—er—Bradford boy friend?

Louise One bloomin' row after another.

George You've obviously got a very quick temper.

Louise That's right.

George What did you throw at the Bradford one?

Louise His trousers, I think.

There is a slight pause

You going to let me have the money then? Just enough to crash out for a couple of nights?

George Well I suppose if you've got nowhere—I must be quite honest though—I don't really believe in—er. It's not that I'm mean. I donate to all sorts of charities.

Louise Well, come on, donate a couple of quid to the Bradford Pudding Club.

George It's ridiculous anyway. Two pounds won't go anywhere.

Louise Make it a fiver then.

George You'd be far wiser to patch up your quarrel with this Davey chap upstairs and stay there until you go into hospital.

Louise Hospital?

George For the baby.

Louise They won't get me into any flaming hospital. You've only got to read the papers. I'd end up with the wrong baby and my appendix out.

George Surely you've made some plans.

Louise (*grinning*) I'm not very good at planning.

George The doctor must have made some plans.

Louise What doctor?

George (*slowly*) Haven't you seen a doctor?

Louise What do I need a doctor for? A bloomin' idiot could tell it's not a carbuncle.

George What a mess.

Louise I don't know why you're so worked up. It isn't due for another eight days.

George Oh, my God!

Louise All the fuss that's made about something as natural as giving birth. It'll be just like shelling peas.

George It'll be *nothing* like shelling peas!

Louise In India the women drop their babies out in the field then go straight back to work, hoeing maize or whatever.

George The point is you're not an Indian woman and you won't be able to carry on like that on Hampstead Heath. You're the most irresponsible person I've ever met. It's criminal irresponsibility. (*Putting his hand to his head*) You're giving me a headache.

Louise Bloody hell you'll give yourself ulcers, you will.

George I've already got them.

Louise Are you married?

George (*after a slight pause*) No.

Louise You have been though, haven't you?

George Yes!

Louise I thought so. You've got that sort of haunted look about you.

The telephone rings and George answers it

George (*on the phone*) Two-three-nine—oh . . . Oh, hullo, Helen . . . Sort what out? . . . Oh—er—yes. . . . No, no trouble. (*He shoots Louise a glance*) She was collecting for a Charity . . . Save the Children Fund.

Louise Hey.

George (*on the phone*) One moment, Helen. (*To Louise, irritably*) What is it?

Louise Can I use your "loo"?

George Must you?

Louise Where else would you suggest?

George All right.

Louise (*pointing to the bedroom*) Is it through there?

George Yes!

Louise Ta.

Louise exits off the bedroom

George (*on the phone*) Sorry about that . . . It was—er—the same lady as before . . . The charity lady, yes . . . No, not collecting this time—delivery . . . my flag. I'm not getting involved, Helen! . . .

Louise enters. During the remainder of the call she wanders through into the kitchen. She tastes the Suki Yaki and likes it

She's gone . . . All right. Is there anything else? . . . Wednesday night, as usual. Of course . . . I'd better ring off now, Helen . . . Of course I'm by myself.

Louise (*calling out*) Can I have some of your Sooky Pooky?

George clamps his hand over the receiver

George (*shouting quietly*) Be quiet!

Louise (*shouting quietly*) Can I have some of your Sooky Pooky?

George Yes. (*On the phone, nonchantly*) I'll ring you in the morning, Helen. Bye.

Louise helps herself to a large plate of food from the various pans. George puts down the phone and joins her, switching off the lounge lights

Louise I liked your loo.

George Good. I'm glad.

Louise Apart from those bloomin' awful rubber plants! The rice goes with this lot, does it?

George It can do. Yes. (*Surveying her plate*) When did you last eat?

Louise Dunno. I think we had some breakfast. Are you going to have any of this stuff?

George If you don't mind.

Louise Help yourself.

George Thank you very much.

She sits at the table but there is not much room because of her stomach

Louise Good thing I'm nice and slim.

George It's probably a bit overcooked now.

Louise No, it's O.K. Do you eat Japanesey all the time?

George Good Lord, no. Once a week I try something a little different, that's all. Tell me—is that flat upstairs on the telephone?

Louise It's all the boys can do to stop them cutting off the gas and electric. What do you want to know for anyway?

George To ring up your friend and tell him he's got to look after you.

Louise I don't need looking after. And I'm not going back up there. Nobody's going to own me.

George Is that what the other fellow did? Tried to own you?

Louise Lad from Bradford.

George Yes.

Louise Suppose so. He didn't know what he wanted to do. There was one thing he did bloody well, I can tell you. (*She pats her tummy*)

George (*trying to ignore it*) Yes, I'm sure.

Louise Hell but he was fruity.

George He was what?

Louise Fruity.

George What does that mean?

Louise Fruity. Randy. He was a right prescription that one.

George (*blankly*) A right prescription?

Louise He liked it three times a day after meals.

George carries on eating, rather embarrassed

　Are *you* fruity?

George Would you like some mango chutney?

Louise Don't think so.

George Home-made.

Louise By you?

George Yes.

Louise Do you knit as well?

George No! They're chopsticks. (*Louise chuckles at him*)

Louise Thought they were early Victorian knitting-needles.

George Oh no, they're chopsticks, all right. They're Chinese—— They really should be Japanese.

Louise (*suddenly*) Ouch! (*She holds her stomach*)

George What is it?

Louise Little basket kicked me.

George Probably disapproves of your conversation at the dinner table.

Louise Oh, you are uptight. Oo! (*She holds her stomach*) There he goes again. Do you want to feel?

George No, thank you. (*He quickly sits and helps himself to chutney*) Haven't you got any relatives or friends you could stay with in London?

Louise No. (*Suddenly*) You're worried about me, aren't you?

George No! It just seems too awful, a young girl leaving here with no arrangements made about hospitals or doctors or anything.

Louise Hey, this is good! You're starting to share my experience.

George I'm not sharing anything! You should have stayed with that boy in Bradford.

Louise Why? He's done his share.

George You must have been fond of him at one time.

Louise Not really. It was just a bit of fun. With a bloke I happened to meet. I didn't want it to last.

George But you're going to have his baby!

Louise So what?!

George Obviously you're one of these young people to whom the conventions of our society mean absolutely . . .

Louise Bugger all—dead right. I think they all should have been buried years ago including Father Christmas, the weatherman and civil servants.

George I'm a civil servant.

Louise (*laughing*) You're not. Of course, you must be. (*Laughing*) What are you in? The Ministry of Pensions?

George Yes.

Louise (*stopping laughing*) I shouldn't laugh.

George Oh, you have got some appreciation of other people's feelings.

Louise No. I'd just hate to laugh so much that I dropped it in your kitchen. What do you do in the Ministry of Pensions? Stick those silly stamps on cards?

George No! I'm what they call a E.O.

Louise E.O.?

George Executive Officer—Grade Two.

Louise Is that good?

George Oh, yes! It's only one step from supervisor. (*Chattily*) Mr Saunders is our supervisor at present. He can be a bit of a tartar, as a matter of fact. Only last Tuesday . . .

Louise How long have you been doing this trip?

George Trip?

Louise The civil servant bit?

George Eighteen years.

Louise Blimey, don't they give you time off for good behaviour? No wonder you're uptight.

George I enjoy the work very much.

Louise Give over.

George No, it's really quite complicated and one has the feeling of job satisfaction. You know, of doing something really worthwhile . . . (*Embarrassed*) Well I enjoy it anyway.

Louise Pensions. National Health, State Hospitals. The Establishment. Crap.

George I wish you wouldn't use words like that.

Louise Establishment?

George No.

Louise What then?

A slight pause

George Crap. I mean why do hippies have to talk like that?

Louise That's about all that upsets you, isn't it? You'll swallow Father Christmas, the Horse Guards Parade and the Ministry of Pensions but somebody says "bum" and you practically die. And I'm not a hippy. Hippies went out with early Victorian crumpet warmers.

George Oh. Well, beatnik, drop-out. Whatever you call yourself. I don't know.

Louise (*angrily*) Why do you have to file everybody? I'm me. I'm doing my own thing—where I want to—and when I want to. I don't need anything from anybody.

George I thought you needed two pounds.

Louise Oh! (*She rises angrily*)

George (*clucking*) Sorry, that was unfair. Really rather hitting below the belt . . . (*He stops as he notices her stomach*)

Louise That stuff wasn't half bad. (*She goes to the fruit bowl, and turns on the lights*)

George (*drily*) I'm glad you liked it. I mean don't bother to say "Thank you!"

She helps herself to a banana

Louise Oh, the polite bit. I gave that up...

George I can see that. Do help yourself to a banana. I suppose good manners are another of the conventions you find so "square".

Louise Good manners mean bugger all.

George reacts momentarily to the swearing

George I'm afraid I don't agree.

Louise My mother and father were so polite to each other it made me sick.

George I'm sorry. I don't understand that.

Louise Because it was phoney. It was always: (*mimicking*) "Sorry *dear*" and, "Oh, no, it was my fault, *sweetheart*". "You shouldn't have done that, *darling*." "Of course I should, you're my *little pet*." All the time my mother was having it off with the next door neighbour.

George Oh. (*At a loss*) That must have been very disturbing.

Louise Not really. Didn't disturb my father much either. He was too busy having it off with the neighbour's wife.

George gives an embarrassed nod of his head

George Well—not everybody carries on like that.

Louise There are three sorts of people. Those who are having it off with their neighbour. Those who wish they were. And those who've got bloody ugly neighbours. Any road, I packed and split. Left them all to it.

George (*after a slight frown*) Haven't you got *any* money at all?

Louise Few bob I think. (*She holds her stomach*) Woops! Another kick! I think he's going to be a bloomin' footballer.

George And you're really setting off by yourself with not the faintest idea where you are going to sleep tonight.

Louise I'll get a place.

George Good God, girl, you may not.

Louise Yes, I will. You just don't know what's going on out there. (*She indicates the world*) There's always some group or other who's got a pad they'll share with you.

George But for heaven's sake, you're nine months pregnant.

Louise Well, it's not bloody catching, is it?

There is a pause

I've got to go now.

George Are you sure you've had enough to eat?

Louise Yes.

There is a fractional pause as George is at a loss

You going to let me have that money, then?

George hesitates, then nods and goes through the lounge and off into the bedroom

Louise, leaving her bag in the kitchen, looks for somewhere to put her half-eaten banana. Finally she puts it back in the fruit bowl

Was that your girlfriend you were talking to on the telephone just now? (*She takes a cigarette from the box*)

George enters with his money

George Good Lord, no. My sister, Helen.
Louise (*surprised*) Your sister?
George Yes.
Louise She goes on a bit, doesn't she?
George She's not very well.
Louise I see.
George (*handing her two five-pound notes*) Here you are.
Louise (*impressed*) Ten quid!
George It's all in a good cause—Save the Children Fund.

She takes it

Louise I helped myself to another fag.
George That's all right. (*Suddenly*) Look, why don't you use that to get up to Bradford. Send your parents a telegram saying you're coming home.
Louise They're busy enough without me turning up.
George In what way?
Louise Keeping the neighbours happy for one thing. Any road, I think they were secretly relieved when I left.
George I'm sure you could go back.
Louise (*defiantly*) But I'm not going to.

The front door bell rings. Louise looks at George, who hesitates

George (*calling*) Who is it?
Davey (*off*) From upstairs.
Louise (*whispering urgently*) It's Davey. Don't let him in.
George (*whispering*) I'll have to.
Louise I won't see him.
George Don't you think . . .
Louise I won't see him.
George You'll have to see him.
Louise I'll wait in your bedroom.
George No!
Louise I'm not going back upstairs.

Louise exits into the bedroom

Davey comes in. He is a young man of about nineteen and much more "Hippy" in appearance than Louise. His long hair is in waves to his shoulders with a band around his head and beads around his neck. He wears a wildly coloured shirt, fanciful trousers, no socks and sandals. He is tall, well set-up and attractive. He could be Scots. His manner is very pleasant which worries George

Davey Hi there, man.

George Oh, hello! That is, hi, man. I'm sorry I took so long answering the door. I was on the telephone—to my sister.

Davey Got the pad above.

George I beg your pardon.

Davey I've got the pad above.

George Oh, yes, *you've* got the—er—pad above. Yes. Quite. Actually, I've—er—passed the time of day with the young man you share with. We've had the—er—odd word together. Nice to meet you. Can I help at all?

Davey (*looking around*) Could be, man. Could be.

George (*making conversation*) It's quite a pleasant neighbourhood this, don't you think?

Davey Yeah.

George I've been meaning to pop up ever since you moved in.

Davey Yep?

George Yes. Just to say hello, mind you. Just to say—hi there, man.

Davey (*quite pleasantly*) Where's our chick?

George Your—er. . . ?

Davey Chick.

George When you say chick, do you mean. . . ?

Davey Come on, man. Give.

George She did call actually. Simply explained you'd had a bit of a tiff and she'd thrown some trousers at you . . .

Davey Record-player.

George Record-player. Trousers, Bradford. She—er—and then—er—left.

Davey No, she didn't. No-one's been through the front door. Been looking from the window.

George You probably missed her.

Davey No, Dad.

Davey sits on the settee

George (*jovially*) Well—if you knew she was here why didn't you pop down sooner.

Davey Waiting.

George What for?

Davey just shrugs

She—er—— She'd prefer not to go back upstairs actually.

Davey She's our chick.

George I think she'd rather not be your chick any longer.

Davey Where is she?

George She's—er—she's in my bedroom.

Davey nods. There is a slight pause

(*Looking at his watch*) It's very late. Actually I was in the middle of washing-up—so if . . .

Davey (*grinning*) Do you know what we call you upstairs?

George (*smiling*) No.

Davey See you going in and out. Nine till five. Real wierdo, you are, man.

George Real wierdo; I see!

Davey We call you "Old tight-arse".

George "Old—er—tight—er—arse." Very good.

Davey (*chuckling*) Every morning. Bowler hat, umbrella. Off you go in your little chariot.

George Little. . . ?

Davey Motor vehicle.

George Oh yes.

Davey Now old "tight-arse" has snatched our chick.

George Old tight-arse hasn't snatched anything and if you're trying to threaten me, young man. . . .

Davey (*surprised*) Threaten? Message from above is peace, man. Peace.

George Oh. Well, I'm delighted you're taking that attitude.

Davey Yep, peace. But she's our chick and if she wants out—(*suddenly smiles*)—*she* tells us and not old tight-arse.

George I would have thought that a travelling record-player was sufficient evidence.

Davey Just a flare-up, chief.

George (*trying to be firm*) She really doesn't want to go back with you. I must say I think it would be wiser if she did—all things considered—but she's a determined young lady.

Davey So she's shacking up with you?

George She's not shacking up with me. She was just about to leave.

Davey Yep. And what about her bread situation?

George Well, I did manage to find her something to eat . . .

Davey Folding stuff, she's got no loot, man.

George Ah, well I've been able to help out a little in that direction. Not much but enough to see her through a few days.

Davey Very cool.

George Well, it's my opinion one ought to try and share these experiences.

There is a pause as they look at each other

Davey See you around, man. . . .

Davey gives a wave, and exits, closing the door himself

George See you around—man. (*He goes to the bedroom door and opens it*) You can come out now, Minnehaha's gone.

Louise enters from the bedroom

Louise Was it O.K?

George We didn't actually finish on "first-name" terms but there seemed a certain friendliness in the way he referred to me as "old tight-arse".

Louise grins

I suppose that's the same as being "uptight".

Louise More or less. What did he say?

George Nothing much. He was rather concerned about your "bread" situation.

Louise Fat lot he could do about it. Did he want me to go back?

George I think that's what he'd prefer.

Louise Yes. Wants to bloody own me.

George Ah, yes, of course! The cardinal sin.

Louise (*after a slight pause*) My bag's in the kitchen. (*She moves towards the kitchen*)

George Hang on a minute!

Louise (*stopping*) What now?

George (*floundering*) Well, it just seems so ridiculous a young girl—I mean, nowhere to—you could walk about half the—I know it's really nothing to do with—and you can please yourself—mind you, I'm not saying—er . . .

Louise What the hell are you talking about?

George Why—why not stay here?

Louise I told you. I'm not going back upstairs.

George No. I mean—here.

Louise (*amazed*) Here?

George Why not? You could get a good night's rest. Have a decent breakfast in the morning and start out nice and fresh.

Louise You're joking.

George No, I'm not.

Louise I don't get it. Half an hour ago all you'd ever done was donate to charity and now suddenly you want to be president of the "Pudding Club".

George It seems a sensible suggestion.

Louise Come on. What's the catch?

George There's no catch.

Louise There must be some catch. (*Suddenly*) You needn't think I'm coming across.

George Coming across what?

Louise Coming across with a bit of the other.

George (*realizing*) That's a ridiculous suggestion. I wouldn't dream of doing anything like that.

Louise Are you homosexual then?

George No! No! (*deeper voice*) No! It just wouldn't enter my head—in your condition.

Louise (*suddenly smiling*) Bloomin' safe, I can tell you that.

George I'm absolutely astonished you can even talk about it.

Louise It's natural, isn't it?

George Of course but, well—like you are.

Louise It's not easy, I admit.

George You mean you've—er . . .

Louise Once or twice.

George (*pompously*) I think that's very silly. It could be dangerous.

Louise You mean a fellow could slip off and break his neck.

George gives her a withering look

George (*coldly*) No, I was thinking of the baby.

Louise You don't read the newspapers at all, do you? Doctors say it's perfectly safe.

George Do they? And do they say anything about the moral issue involved in that sort of behaviour?

Louise (*angrily*) Now that's e-bloody-nough! You've been asking questions all night and you've had your pissy moneysworth!

George Charming!

Louise You know what you are, don't you. You're a hypocrite. A pompous, prissy hypocritical old pouffe!

George And you're a damn spoiled little brat. No wonder your parents were glad to get rid of you.

Louise (*stung*) They weren't glad to get rid of me. I didn't say that. My folks love me. They'd be glad to take me back.

George But you wouldn't want to go back. They're just a couple of phonies and you're much too honest for them. The whole world's phony, isn't it?

Louise And you're the pick of the bunch!

Louise marches into the kitchen to collect her bag. George follows her

George You know it all, don't you?

Louise I know a bloody sight more than you do. I've lived my life. I won't end up in the Ministry of Pensions.

George You've already ended up in the Ministry of Labour!

Louise You've got sex on the brain, you have. Probably because you're no good at it. I'll bet that's why your wife walked out on you. Like doing it with a bloomin' computer.

George Now, dammit, that's enough. You get out of here. I wouldn't let you stay in my flat now if you were having quintuplets.

Louise Don't worry, I'm going. I don't want to stay cooped up in this blinking junk shop. And you can have this back, too. (*She throws the ten pounds at him*) I don't want anything from you. You don't know how to share. You can stick your money and your flat right up your tight . . .

George Out!

Louise exits

George closes the door and picks up the ten pounds

(*To himself*) Charming. Absolutely charming.

George goes through into the kitchen and starts to run water on to dirty crockery. For the next minute or so he proceeds to talk to himself complaining about Louise and enacting her behaviour. He finds the half-eaten banana and throws it away. Finally, the door bell goes. He hesitates, looks at his watch, then dries his hands and opens the door

Louise comes in, with a slightly bewildered look on her face

George (*tensely*) Have you forgotten something?
Louise I had a pain.

George looks worried and helps her to the settee

George Oh no! A bad one?
Louise So-so.
George Oh dear, I'm so sorry. Are you all right? How is it now? Gone?
Louise I think so—yes.

She sinks down gratefully on settee. There is a tense pause as George watches her anxiously. Slowly she relaxes and smiles

George You don't think it's time, do you?
Louise No. Another eight days yet.
George (*irritably*) It could be premature, you know.
Louise Better not be. If it is I'll bang it on the head and send it back. No, this was just a pain. You get proper advance warnings.
George What are you expecting, a notice through the post?
Louise I'm all right now. I'll go in a minute.
George (*firmly*) Oh, no you won't. You're staying here tonight. I'll get you a glass of water.

George goes through into kitchen. Louise hesitates a moment, her bravado gone

Louise (*calling out*) I'm sorry.
George That's all right.
Louise I'll be O.K. in a bit. Honest.
George Here, drink this up—it'll do you good.

He returns and gives her the glass of water. She drinks it down. George takes the ten pounds out of his pocket

George You better have this back. You'll need it first thing tomorrow. (*He puts it in her bag*)
Louise Can I have a fag?
George Don't you think you've smoked enough?

She stops him with a reproving look

Help yourself.

She helps herself to a cigarette; whereupon George lights it for her

Louise Aren't you having one?
George I don't smoke.
Louise You just keep these for unmarried mothers, do you?

George (*almost smiling*) No.

Louise You'd be surprised how many you'd get through.

George I keep them, for some of the chaps from the office. Four of us play bridge here once a month.

Louise I'll ring the vice squad right away.

George (*conversationally*) We—er—we play once a week actually and take it in turns to act as host. That means my—er—turn comes round . . .

Louise Once a month, yes. Do you cook for them?

George Yes. Yes, I do. They seem to like my cooking. Last time I gave then Bisque d'Hommard, Coq au Vin and—jelly. You're going to stay tonight, aren't you? Please be sensible. You can leave first thing in the morning after breakfast.

Louise gets up and moves away

If it'll make you feel any easier you can have the place to yourself.

Louise (*turning to him*) Don't be silly . . .

George My sister could put me up for the night. She's not far away.

Louise I can imagine.

George Shall I give her a ring?

Louise Not bloody likely.

George I just thought it might look better if I didn't stay here with you.

Louise (*suddenly softer*) If I *do* stay—I'd rather *you* did, too.

George Would you? Really?

Louise Not half. It would give me the horrors being alone in this place.

George looks disappointed for a moment then quickly pulls himself together, gets very business-like

George I see. Good, that's settled. Early night for you. You can have my bed and I'll have the put-u-up in here.

George starts to turn the put-u-up down

Louise No. I'd rather sleep in here.

George Why?

Louise To be near the door just in case.

George Please yourself. It's jolly comfortable.

Louise Have you slept on it then?

George Not recently. I used to—now and then.

Louise When you were married?

George I thought I was the one who asked too many questions.

Louise Is that what used to happen, though? You'd get too fruity and she'd banish you to the put-u-up.

George No. How many pillows would you like? One or two?

Louise I haven't been having that sort of luxury lately.

George I've got plenty. Two?

Louise Three.

George Three! Oh my goodness. I don't know whether I have three matching pillow-slips. (*He goes towards the bedroom with a smile, then stops*) I'm sorry—I just realized: I don't know your name.

Louise Louise. Louise Hamilton. They call me "big Louie".
George I'd rather call you Louise. I'm George.
Louise Yes, you look like a "George". What's your last name, "Smith"?
George No, "Clarke".

George exits into the bedroom

Louise is now much more relaxed

Louise (*calling*) What do you drink at night? I'll make it.
George (*off*) Drink. I really don't mind. What do *you* drink?
Louise Coke.
George (*off*) Well, tonight it's cocoa.

George enters with bedding

The phone rings. He stops and hesitates

I expect that'll be Helen.
Louise What is she, a telephone operator?
George Probably ringing up to say "Good night".

Louise picks up the phone

Louise (*on the phone, huskily*) Not now, darling, we're busy.

George looks absolutely horrified as she puts the phone down. Louise is delighted with her piece of devilment and goes into the kitchen to prepare the cocoa. She puts milk into the saucepan

George (*following her*) That was very silly. She'll be worried stiff, you know.
Louise (*putting the saucepan on the gas*) She ought to be tickled pink. Where's the cocoa?
George In the cupboard. Why should she be tickled pink?
Louise That you might be getting your oats with some dolly bird.
George She'll probably send the police round or something.

George starts to put the put-u-up down

Louise Is she married?
George No.
Louise Never?
George No. She was engaged once. It didn't work. I worry. She isn't too well.
Louise Do we need sugar in this?
George Yes please. I'd like one level teaspoon. Anyhow, I feel sort of responsible for her. Actually she's a couple of years older than I am. I look in on her as often as possible. We chat on the phone.
Louise Chat?
George Yes, we chat! And we have dinner together on Wednesday evenings. One week her place, the next mine.

Louise *Every* Wednesday.

George Yes. Every Wednesday.

Louise Live dangerously next week—make it Tuesday.

George (*seriously*) I couldn't do that. Tuesday's bridge night.

Louise (*chuckling at him*) Wow!

The phone rings again. There is a slight pause as George and Louise look at each other. Louise teasingly makes a quick move as though to rush and answer it. George dashes through and picks up the phone

George (*on the phone*) Two-three-nine—oh . . . (*In mock surprise*) Hullo, Helen . . . Girl? What girl? . . . No. You must have dialled the wrong number by mistake. Anyway, what can I do for you? . . .

Louise comes in and puts the two cups of cocoa on table in the kitchen

Couple of aspirins will probably do the trick . . . Well, I hope you'll feel better in the morning. I'll ring you from the office . . . Good night, Helen . . . Yes. Good night.

Louise takes the phone from him and blows several quick kisses into the receiver. George snatches it back

(*On the phone*) Good night, Helen . . . What noise? Just blowing you some kisses . . . Not a drop, honestly . . . I'm fine, really I am. Good night, sleep tight.

Louise Hope the bugs don't bite!

George (*on the phone*) Hope the bugs don't . . . Good night, God bless!

He puts the phone down and glares at Louise. Louise smiles and shrugs

Are you like that all the time?

Louise (*overacting*) No, kid. Only when I've had my shot. (*She mimes a "shot" in the arm*)

George (*horrified*) You don't take drugs do you?

Louise (*playing up*) Half-a-pound a day. What's the time.

George Half-past nine.

Louise Half-past nine? I've got to have a fix!

She lays on her back, and kicks her legs. George realizes she's joking, gets up and walks away

George Very funny—no, it's not funny. I know a lot of young people *do* take drugs nowadays. I read it in the *Observer*.

Louise I tried drugs once. Back in Bradford.

George (*surprised*) Bradford?

Louise Yes, Bradford. (*Sarcastically*) They have talking-pictures there as well, you know. Any road, I didn't like it. I had a bit of a bad trip.

George Good Lord, weren't you afraid to take it?

Louise Afraid?

George Of what might happen?

Louise I was more afraid not to. I might have missed something, understand?

George I don't think I do, no. How about those young men upstairs? I suppose they—er . . .

Louise (*off-hand*) Oh we smoke grass sometimes, that's all.

George (*blankly*) You smoke grass?

Louise Marijuana. When we could get it. But that's nothing.

George Nothing!

Louise It's O.K. I don't have any on me. You don't have to worry about a raid. Stick 'em up. (*She imitates frisking*)

George (*smiling*) Golly, you're a funny mixture.

Louise I know. Gemini.

George (*Sitting*) Gemini?

Louise Gemini. That's the star I was born under. The twins. Temperamental. One moment happy. (*She does a silly laugh*) One moment miserable. (*She pulls a long face*)

George We're all like that.

Louise Are *you*?

George Yes.

Louise You don't seem it. You seem—in control.

George I see, yes.

Louise Let's have our cocoa. (*She sips her cocoa*) Tastes like hot sick!

This is too much for George who puts his cocoa down and gets on with making the bed

Louise Hey, George?

George What is it?

Louise I enjoyed the row we had earlier, didn't you?

George Yes, I . . . (*Realising*) No, I didn't.

Louise Why not? (*She helps him make the bed*)

George I don't know. I don't like getting upset. I don't think I've ever had a shouting match like that before.

Louise I have them all the bloody time.

George Yes. I wish you wouldn't swear so much.

Louise Why not?

George Well, it doesn't sound very nice.

Louise It's real. It means something. You can stuff your "super" and your "jolly good" and your "hard cheese". My father was always saying "hard cheese". Do you say "hard cheese"?

George Sometimes.

Louise What's it mean?

George I haven't the faintest idea.

Louise I can just imagine what goes on in your office. Some bloke comes in and says, "I say can I have a word with Mr Clarke, B.O. Grade Two . . ."

George *E*.O. B.O.'s a nasty smell.

Louise "I say, Mr Clarke, my insurance card has got two stamps missing. Am I out of benefit?" "I'm afraid you are, old boy. See the Supervisor, old boy. Hard cheese, old boy."

George That's nothing like what happens.

Louise Bet it is.

George No. I mean if someone had two stamps missing from their insurance card they wouldn't necessarily be out of benefit—unless the stamps they *did* have weren't of sufficient value in the first place.

Louise laughs

Louise You're priceless.

George I'm glad you think so.

Louise Piss-elegant but priceless.

George I don't know where you get half these expressions from.

Louise I swear less the more you get to know me.

George That's encouraging.

Louise My basic trouble is I'm shy.

George Shy!

George straightens up from making the bed with a pained look of disbelief

Louise No. I am. Half the time I'm only saying "bloody" or "bugger" or "bum" or "balls" . . .

George Don't give me a list!

Louise Half the time I'm only saying them out of nerves.

George Nerves, I see. (*Finishing the bed*) There we are. Tuck in that end, will you? I think you'd have done better if you'd done hospital comers! Now I'd better find something for you to sleep in.

Louise It's O.K. I sleep naked.

George Oh. Well, don't you think—under the circumstances—you ought to wear something tonight?

Louise Why? You expecting visitors?

George No, but in the morning, I'll be coming through. I think I'd better find you something.

Louise Please yourself. Do you have a small tent about the place?

George You're not all that big.

Louise You should see me when I'm not pregnant. I only weigh seven-and-a-half stone.

There is a slight pause

George I'll get you a pair of my pyjamas.

Louise Thanks.

George Be careful. Your manners are showing.

George exits into the bedroom

Louise sits down, takes her sandals off, and wriggles her toes

George returns with a very ordinary pair of pyjamas, which he hands to her

I got these out of the airing cupboard. I think you'll find them nice and warm.

Louise (*surveying them*) Blimey! I'll be safe in these.

George You'll be safe anyway. You can change in my bedroom.
Louise George?
George Yes?
Louise (*mischievously*) Have you ever lent your pyjamas to any other girl?
George No.
Louise When did you last have a woman here?
George When my mother came to visit me!
Louise Bloody hell, you haven't got a mother as well as a sister?

George takes her towards the bedroom door

George Get changed.
Louise How often does your mother ring up?
George Not often. She lives in Bournemouth.
Louise Bournemouth! Bloody hell!
George Just get changed.

George gently pushes her into the bedroom

   Louise exits

*George picks up the cocoa cups, goes to sip his, but remembers her remark
and takes the cups through to the sink. He picks up the empty milk bottle,
rinses it out, then suddenly gets a thought and goes towards the bedroom door*

   (*Calling*) Louise, shall I. . . ?
Louise (*off, yelling*) Don't come in!
George I won't.
Louise (*off*) Hell, I look awful in these pyjamas!
George You'll be all right.
Louise (*off*) I look like a constipated duck!
George Shall I order some extra milk for the morning?
Louise (*off*) I don't drink that crappy stuff.
George Well, I'm not asking the milkman to leave Coca Cola. (*He gets
pen and paper from the bookshelf*)
Louise (*off*) I don't want any milk, anyway.
George I'll order an extra pint just in case—always comes in handy for
blancmange. (*He starts to write out the milk order*)

   Louise enters behind him, looking very sorrowful in his pyjamas

George finally turns to see her, and can only just stop himself from laughing

Louise If you laugh I'll take them off.

George's face goes blank

George They're—very nice.

She gets into bed and pulls the bedclothes up to her chin

   I'll leave this for the milkman. I'll order some yoghourt as well.
Louise (*sitting up*) Yoghourt?

George Very good for babies.
Louise Lovely. Find some and give it to them.

George puts the milk bottle outside the door. He then closes the front door

George Right. That's fine, then. That's that. Anything else?
Louise Why did your wife leave you?

George hesitates

George Oh. You know. One of those things. (*He starts to tidy up by collecting the two empty whisky glasses*)
Louise I suppose it was sex, was it?
George (*going to the sink*) Just you concentrate on getting a good night's sleep.
Louise Don't you want to talk about it? All right. We won't talk about it.

George returns and collects the ashtray from the table behind the settee and then ashtray from the table L of the settee

Was it sex?

George glares at her

Hell, I'm only asking. If you don't want to tell me, say: "Mind your own business."
George Mind your own business.
Louise Uptight bugger.
George She left me because she stopped being in love with me.
Louise Did you give her cocoa in bed?
George Tea actually.
Louise But you didn't give her "other things in bed". Was that it?
George (*after a pause*) I think she thought—oh, it doesn't matter.
Louise She thought what?
George She thought I—I wasn't—very good at it.
Louise Were you?
George I don't know. I certainly never got any prizes for it.
Louise (*pressing on*) Was it that you couldn't manage it or that when you did you couldn't . . .
George Louise, please!
Louise Well, if she was too fruity for you . . .
George Please! I don't want to talk about it. (*He turns out the kitchen light*)
Louise That's your trouble.
George Yes, I know. Uptight. Very appropriate. Do *you* think I'd be difficult to live with? (*He turns on the table lamp beside the settee*)
Louise If you couldn't manage to give it to me, bloody difficult!

George turns out all the lights except one behind the settee and the standard lamp

George Well it wasn't as bad as all that. It didn't govern our whole lives. Good Lord, it isn't *that* important.

Louise It's hard to think of what comes bloody second!
George Anyway we had plenty of other things in common.
Louise I'm pleased to hear it.

George sits on the edge of the bed

George Walking. Bridge. And we were both very fond of scrabble. It seemed like a reasonably good life. But one day we had this—it was just a tiny argument—I mean it was nothing like us just now. And all of a sudden in the middle of this—tiny little argument—she said she was going to leave me.
Louise (*quietly*) What was the argument about?
George Sugar.
Louise (*surprised*) Sugar?
George We—er—we always had a cup of tea together in the afternoon when I got back from the office. It was a sort of ritual, you know. And I always made it—I liked to—she'd been stuck in all day, you see. Well, this particular afternoon I gave her her cup, she tasted it and said: "You've only put one lump in." Now, I wouldn't make a mistake like that. "I've put two lumps in as usual", I said. "You can't have stirred it properly." And she said: "George. I can't live with you any more."
Louise (*after a long pause*) I don t think she left you because of the sugar. Did you have any children?
George No. I wanted to but I suppose it's just as well. I heard she got married again. I sort of vaguely know the chap. Very unreliable sort. Drinks a bit, too. Belligerent, rather. Still, she can live with him—and she couldn't live with me. That's what I don't understand. Can you understand that?

Louise can, but she remains silent. George pulls himself together, turns out the standard lamp, then moves above the bed

(*Indicating the lamp on the table above the bed*) I'll leave this light on. (*He goes towards the bedroom*) Good night, then, Louise. Sleep tight.
Louise George?
George Hm?
Louise Maybe it wasn't all your fault, you know.
George What wasn't?
Louise (*quietly*) Sometimes a girl can put a fellow off. You know, scare him a bit. If she's not—gentle enough. Or—yielding enough . . .
George (*quickly*) I'll see you in the morning.

George scuttles into the bedroom

Louise smiles to herself then gives a contented smile, turns off the light and settles down in bed. After a few seconds the light goes on again and Louise is sitting up in bed with a pained look on her face and clutching her stomach. It is important that, during the whole of the ensuing scene until the end of the act, Louise does not get frightened or upset. The labour pains make her more furious than anything else, and, in fact, she enjoys the experience of it all

Louise Oh! (*To herself*) Oh bloody hell. Oh, bugger, I think this is it. (*She calls out*) Fred! Bert! Whatever your name is. George!

George hurries in from the bedroom and puts the kitchen light on

George All right. All right. What on earth's the matter?
Louise I think it's coming.
George What is?
Louise Well not Christmas, you daft bugger.
George God, you mean, the baby? But it can't. It's not due for eight days.

George rushes upstage and puts the lounge lights on. Louise relaxes slightly, the pain having gone

Louise I haven't had that sort of pain before. This is it, lad.
George How long do you think you've got?
Louise I don't know.
George (*panicking*) All right now. You're going to be fine. You mustn't get excited. It won't help to get excited. Do you want anything—a sandwich or a piece of cake? Cup of tea?

She shakes her head

No. Well, the first thing to do is—er—what the hell, what is the first thing to do? Hospital! I'll get you to hospital right away. Now just you relax. (*Moving to the bedroom*) I'll get the car keys.
Louise No.
George The car's right outside. We'll be there in five minutes. Hampstead General.
Louise No, I won't go there.
George Louise, that's the place to have a baby.
Louise I hate hospitals.
George So do I! I really do but when I have a baby that's where I'll go.
Louise Well, I won't. I hate them.
George Why for heaven's sake?
Louise They're so bloomin' antiseptic!
George That's the whole point!
Louise They don't care about you. They're phony.
George This is no time to fight the Establishment.

Louise gets another pain

Louise Wah-oo!
George Now will you go to hospital?

Louise gritting her teeth, shakes her head

Louise, you're a silly stubborn girl! I want to help you. Understand?

Louise nods

All right. Now—whether you like it or not—people do believe a hospital is the best place to have a baby. Right? So you'll go, won't you?

Louise shakes her head

Why not, for heaven's sake?

Louise's pain has gone and she smiles

Louise I want my baby to have a natural birth.

George Well, have a natural birth in hospital. I'll tell the sister personally. I'll say: "Please let Miss Hamilton have a lovely natural birth."

Louise I want it here. Can't you understand? I don't want the Establishment bit. I don't want the white coats and the oxygen and all that crap. It's my own thing.

George (*walking away*) She's mad as a hatter.

Louise (*getting a pain*) Wah-hoo!

George (*jumping*) Ah! You won't go to hospital.

She shakes her head

All right. I'll go and get a doctor. (*He moves to front door*)

Louise George!

George For God's sake! Surely a doctor's all right? I'll find one who's not too antiseptic. You can have a nice natural birth. "Your own thing" with no oxygen, no white coats and absolutely no crap at all. (*He moves to the door*)

Louise Don't leave me.

George I'll only be ten minutes or so. There's nothing to be scared about.

Louise I'm not scared. I just want you to stay with me.

George I've got to get a doctor!

Louise George!

George What is it?

Louise Phone for one.

George Louise . . .

Louise Phone for one. It's quicker.

George Yes, you're right. (*He hurries to the phone and suddenly stops*) I don't know any doctors.

Louise Haven't *you* got a doctor?

George I suppose so, yes. I rarely go. I'm with a group. Three or four of them. They sound something like Freeman, Hardy and Willis. I can never remember my one's name. I know he's not the first one. (*George picks up the yellow telephone book*) The yellow pages. I'll look under "Doctors" and find one with a Hampstead address. I mean anyone'll do.

Louise gets another pain

Louise Wah-hoo! Bloody hell! Oh, bugger me!

George That's it. You swear as much as you like. Don't mind me.

Louise Bloody buggering hell!

George Jolly good. You bloody buggering hell as much as you like. I can't find "Doctors" anywhere. (*He reads*) "Detergents", "Dish Washing", "Deep Sea Divers", "Dog Foods", "Dog Grooming", "Dog Kennels" . . .

Louise If I were a pregnant poodle I'd be fine.

George Here we are! "Doctors." "For Doctors see under Physicians and Surgeons." It would have been just as easy to put them under Doctors.

Louise's pain subsides. George is frantically looking under "Doctors"

Louise I'm terribly sorry.

George (*without looking up*) What?

Louise I'm terribly sorry about landing you in all this.

George (*without looking up*) Oh, that's all right. I wasn't doing anything else tonight.

Louise Can't you find a doctor?

George Pages of them but not one with a Hampstead address. Amazing, isn't it? You go for a walk on the Heath and you'll bump into twenty doctors. (*He reads*) Shepherd's Bush. Shepherd's Bush. Why do they want so many doctors in Shepherd's Bush.

Louise gets another pain

Louise Bloody hell!

George hurries over to her

George All right?

Louise's face is screwed up

Louise Bloody hell!

George Are they getting worse?

Louise nods

Bloody hell! (*He starts to go back to the phone book*)

Louise Hey, I had this girl friend in Bradford who got pregnant. She said she used to sing while she was getting the labour pains.

George (*not listening*) Sing, did she? Gosh, that must have been fun. (*Reading*) Shepherd's Bush. Shepherd's Bush. God, that must be an unhealthy place. Ah, thank God, Hampstead, N.W. three. Dr Fitch. Four-three-five oh-double-eight two.

Louise I'm going to try that on the next one.

George Try what?

Louise Singing. (*She gets a pain*) Ahh!

Louise starts to sing. The pain is quite bad and she is singing loudly and intently to counteract it

(*Singing*) "Ahhf a pound of tuppenny rice, half a pound of treacle, etc."

George puts the book down

George You'll be all right. Don't worry.

Louise grabs his hand

(*Shouting*) I'll ring this Dr Fitch and get him here, right away.

George moves to go, but cannot because she has got his hand in a vice-like grip. He ends up across the bed with a wrestling 'back hammer' grip on.

Louise, my hand—I can't reach—my hand . . .
Louise Oh 'ell! (*Singing*) " 'Oel, 'Oel, 'Oel.
                                        Born is the King of Israel!"

George lays there foolishly, until her pain subsides

George What did you say the singing was supposed to do?
Louise I'm not quite sure. Puts your mind on something else. It seemed to help. Join in next time.

George grabs the telephone and starts to dial. Louise starts to give a little giggle

Louise (*laughing*) It just struck me.
George (*without looking up*) What did?
Louise (*laughing*) If this had been Tuesday—(*she laughs even more*)—we'd have had your bridge party going on.

George gives her a quick glare

Louise (*getting a pain*) Wah-hoo!
George Oh, God!

Louise starts singing: "When the Saints go marching in"

(*On the phone*) Dr Fitch please . . . Oh, thank heavens. My name's Clarke. George Clarke. Could you call right away please and deliver a baby? . . . Flat number two. Twenty-five Millington Ave . . . Yes . . . Well, she seems to be having pains . . . At the moment? She's singing . . . I beg your pardon . . . I haven't the faintest idea. (*To Louise*) He wants to know if your water's broken or something.
Louise What is he, a plumber?
George (*on the phone*) No, there's no midwife, just me . . . Oh, dear. How long will you be? . . . Ten minutes . . . Oh good.
Louise (*getting a pain*) Wah-hoo!
George (*on the phone*) Could you make it five? . . . Sheets . . . Boiling water . . . Towels . . . What do you mean, if you don't get here in time? . . . I will? . . . Don't talk any more, just hurry.

George puts the phone down, hurries into kitchen and puts kettle of water on gas while Louise continues to sing: "When the Saints go marching in"

I'll boil some water. (*Calling from the kitchen*) You'll be all right. The doctor's coming round immediately. He says you've probably got plenty of time yet. Just relax. You'll be fine until your water breaks. That's a sign apparently that things are beginning to happen. Nothing's broken yet, has it?

Louise, still singing, shakes her head

Jolly good. Jolly good.

George hurries through into the bedroom, returning almost immediately with a bath-towel and two sheets that he has obviously just pulled off his bed, a plastic bucket and a 'squeegy'. The telephone rings and George quickly picks it up

(*On the phone*) Two-three-nine-oh . . . Oh, no! Helen, I can't talk now. I'm having a baby! You'll have to ring back . . .

Louise stops singing

Louise George!
George (*to Louise*) What is it?
Louise I'm soaking wet!
George (*on the phone*) I've got to ring off. We've had a birth . . .

George puts the phone down. He rushes over to Louise and holds her tight. They both start singing: "When the Saints . . ." very loudly, as—

the CURTAIN *falls*

ACT II

SCENE 1

The same. Ten days later, 5.30 p.m.

The curtains are open and the late afternoon sun is shining in. The room has lost its immaculate appearance and there is a certain amount of disarray, a more "lived-in" look. In the bay-window corner is a new baby's pram. A line of nappies is strung across the kitchen. There are several baby toys around.

Louise enters from the bedroom. She looks back in to check if the baby is asleep and then she looks exhausted with her hair damp and stringy. She wears a denim suit. From upstairs comes the sound of a guitar and then a boy and a girl laughing and singing. She looks up and then gets a cigarette. As she is about to light it the phone rings. She pulls a face and picks up the telephone

Louise (*on the phone*) Hullo, Helen! . . . No, he's not. He should be back any minute. Is there a message? . . . Oh. (*She looks at the phone. Helen having obviously rung off curtly. To the phone*) Good afternoon to you too. (*She puts the phone down and lights the cigarette*)

George enters from the front door carrying an armload of parcels and bags, including a large grocery bag, a bottle of champagne in a carrier bag, a large chemist's bag, a "boutique" bag, a pair of large scales and a baby's measuring stick. He wears the dark suit but a slightly gayer tie and seems altogether lighter in mood

George Hullo, there.

Louise gives a noncommittal wave

How do you feel?
Louise Bloody awful.
George Jolly good.
Louise What have you come as, Father Christmas?

George unloads the parcels

George I've done a bit of shopping. Left the office an hour early.
Louise That'll be on the news tonight.

George smiles. He hears the guitar as the volume increases slightly

George (*pleasantly*) Someone else must have moved in with them up there. Haven't heard the jolly old guitar before.

Louise Been playing the ruddy thing on and off all afternoon.
George Sounds rather nice.
Louise Better not wake the baby.
George And how *is* my little juicy chops? (*He indicates the bedroom*)
Louise He's O.K.

George starts to go towards the bedroom

(*Sharply*) Don't open that door.
George Is he asleep?
Louise Finally. Now he's got his belly full.
George Bless him.
Louise Bless him? It's amazing the damage he can do without teeth.
George Is he covered up all right?

The guitar music stops

Louise No, he's stark naked with the window open.

George moves into the bedroom but stops on realizing she's being sarcastic. He starts to unpack the parcels

(*Chuckling*) You should have seen Mr Saunders' face when I said I was leaving early in order to buy nappies and a nice new potty. (*He gets the potty out of the carrier*)
Louise You daft thing. He'll be at least two months old before he sits on a potty.
George (*disappointed*) Oh, will he?
Louise He'll fall in that and break his neck.
George Oh. Well, it'll keep. (*He puts it back into the bag*) Well now, what's happened today. Anything exciting?
Louise Not half! I was forgetting!
George What?
Louise (*sarcastically*) Your sister phoned.
George Oh. When?
Louise Just now.
George What did she say?
Louise Nothing.
George Is that all?
Louise I said you weren't in, and she hung up in my face.
George Jolly good.
Louise What have you told her about me?
George Nothing, really.
Louise Nothing? You've spoken to her three times a day every day since I've been here. She knows I'm staying here with you, doesn't she?
George Not really. I think she's sort of gathered that you're around the place. (*He starts to take the nappies off the line*)
Louise What about the baby?
George She sort of knows about him.
Louise Well what does she think, that you've opened a maternity home?
George I don't know what she thinks. We don't discuss it.

Louise Bonkers, the pair of you. The only real thing that's happened to you in years and you don't even discuss it with your own sister.

George She wouldn't understand. And I wouldn't know how to tell her about it anyway.

Louise Tell about what for God's sake?

George You—and the baby—and you both staying here.

Louise What do you mean? It's all as pure as the driven snow, isn't it?

George Of course but—you know, it looks, I mean it could look . . .

Louise So you don't tell her anything and she doesn't ask any questions but she knows. And you know she knows. And she knows you know she knows. You both ought to be locked away.

George There's no point in upsetting her, is there?

Louise Yes, she's bloody jealous, that's her trouble.

George Of course she's not.

Louise She's frightened I'll come between the three of you.

George Three of us?

Louise You, her and the telephone. You should tell her outright. "I've got a girl living with me and if you don't like it, hard cheese, bugger you." Haven't you got the guts?

George (*smiling*) No. Anyway, I gather she didn't say why she phoned.

Louise No. Probably wanted to tell you all about her gall bladder.

George There's nothing wrong with her gall bladder. Is there?

Louise Dunno but she's covered everything else. Here, when she's gone through all her parts once, does she start at the beginning again?

George (*ignoring this*) I think I got everything that was on the list. Cotton wool. Soap. Nappy rash ointment, dill water.

Louise (*suspiciously*) What's all this other stuff?

George (*evasively*) I got a few things. Just in case.

Louise *What* things?

George Now don't get perturbed. I've bought the ingredients for bottle feeding.

Louise I've told you before, he doesn't need any bottle feeding.

George It won't hurt to have it ready. These are bottles and teats, and these are the mixtures.

Louise You know what you can do with your bottles and teats and mixtures.

George Louise, please . . .

Louise He's not going to be a bottle baby.

George There's nothing wrong with it. I was a bottle baby.

Louise (*derisively*) Bloody hell!

George Will you listen to reason? You've got to stop wearing yourself out like this. It's nearly a fortnight now. Up at all hours of the night and everything. There's no sense in getting all run down and irritable.

Louise It's not him that makes me irritable, it's you!

George Me?

Louise Yes, you. You're a proper fussy-arse.

George I thought I was a tight-arse.

Louise You're both.

George Maybe I am but you've got to take care of yourself. It's still early days. Now, there's no harm in giving him a bottle once in a while. Say the night feed. I'll prepare it. Have him in here with me and give it to him.

Louise I think you've got a false pregnancy, that's your trouble.

George Just the night feed, that's all.

Louise I said no. Look, who had this baby, you or me?

George After six choruses of "When the Saints come marching home", I think he's partly mine.

Louise That doesn't give you the right to tell me what to do.

George You don't have to take my word for it. Dr Fitch said a bottle a day would be perfectly all right.

He takes the baby's packages through to the kitchen. Louise follows him. During the ensuing dialogue he puts the baby's packages away

Louise (*interrupting him*) Whatever the baby gets, he's going to get it from me. And you can throw those pissy-arse plastic bottles in the dustbin.

George I thought you only swore when you were nervous.

Louise I swear when I'm angry, too. If babies had been meant to have it out of bottles I'd have a couple of bottles here. (*She points to her breasts*)

George runs a weary hand over his forehead

Don't you understand anything about "contact". That's what he wants. Contact and love. And he'll need as much as he can get if he's going to grow up in this phony world.

George starts to put the packages in a cupboard

George Oh, it's not a bad old world.

Louise It's a phony, plastic, disposable world.

George You're getting yourself all tired and run-down. Why don't you take a little nap?

Louise I don't want a "little nap". And I'm not tired and run-down. I'm bloody happy.

George Good.

Louise Or I would be if it wasn't such a phony, plastic, establishment world.

George Well, it's the only one we've got.

George goes through to the lounge and collects the grocery bag. During the ensuing dialogue he unpacks the bag and puts everything away except the steak and the grapefruit

Louise Nothing's for real. Plastic this. Synthetic that. Everything's phony. That Dr Fitch is a right phony. The way he pretends we're married. (*Mimicking him*) "And how are we this morning, Mrs Clarke?"

George I think it's rather sweet.

Louise "He's a fine little chap, Mrs Clarke." My name is Louise Hamilton.

George I think you straightened him out on that point.

Louise Too bloody true. Why can't he just say, "How are you, Miss Hamilton?" He's a fine little basket, Miss Hamilton." I wish he'd stop sticking his nose in here.

George I expect the feeling's mutual. I shouldn't think he's had many patients who've told him to piss off.

George chuckles at the thought of it

Louise What's so funny?

George I was just remembering the expression on his face when you said it to him.

Louise You wouldn't be so bloomin' cheerful if *you* had that baby.

George I've always heard people say that motherhood is an exhilarating experience.

Louise What people, the Pope?

George I suppose it all depends whether the mother in question is ready for motherhood.

Louise What's that supposed to mean?

George It means you feel trapped now and you're taking it out on yourself and the baby.

Louise Blimey first it's Doctor Spock, now it's Professor Freud.

George That's why you won't leave the flat—even for a moment to get some fresh air. You've got to spend every minute feeding the baby and loving it to death.

Louise Well if I am trapped—you've bloody trapped me.

George *I* have? (*He goes into lounge, collects the champagne and returns to the kitchen*)

Louise Yes! You've got me nicely stuck here, haven't you? Me and the baby. Suits you fine, doesn't it?

George goes into the lounge, collects the scales and measuring stick and returns

Fuss, fuss, fuss. You and your fussing—you're like a mother hen. "Cluck, cluck, cluck." That's what you've got to have, someone to fuss over. You like to keep busy that way so you won't have to look at yourself.

George (*thoughtfully weighing this*) That's an interesting thought.

Louise Yeah. Stick that in your office file and analyse it in your tea break.

George Thank you.

Louise You're welcome. (*Her anger begins to cool*) Now we're even.

George Yes. (*He unpacks the scales and measuring stick*)

Louise What's that?

George Scales. For the baby.

Louise (*gently laughing*) For the. . . ? You are daft.

George And this is for measuring him.

Louise Stuff him and we could probably get fifty pence a pound for him.

George It'll be nice to know if he's making proper progress. He was eighteen inches long and five pounds ten ounces at birth.

Louise He was bloody ugly too.

George He wasn't.

Louise He was, too.

George It says in that medical book most babies are sort of blotchy at first.

Louise Blotchy and ugly and skinny.

George Not skinny.

Louise He is skinny. He's so skinny he'll have to run about in the shower to get wet.

George Oh yes! That's very funny. I like that. (*Suddenly*) I had an idea while I was shopping.

Louise What's that?

George We're going to have a celebration tonight.

Louise Celebration.

George Don't you know what day it is?

Louise No.

George It's his birthday.

Louise Birthday?

George Ten days old today.

Louise You can't celebrate ten days.

George I can.

The sun has finally set outside and the glow fades from the windows

I thought we'd have a special birthday dinner! Steak! (*He produces two steaks*)

Louise (*pointing to the bedroom*) That's a smashing birthday treat for him.

George He gets his fair share of treats. It's your turn now. (*He takes her through to the lounge, talking as he goes*) Off you go now. Just go and get changed.

Louise George, look . . .

George No arguments.

Louise George!

George Fussy-arse is in charge now.

Louise Don't be silly.

George You slip into something more relaxing.

Louise The only more relaxing thing I've got is a pair of your pyjamas.

George (*overacting*) Of course! I was forgetting. (*He picks up large boutique carrier bag*) Happy birthday!

He holds out the carrier bag and Louise stands there looking at him for a moment. George's bravado deserts him

If you don't like it you can change it.

Louise takes out the dress, which can be a gay coulette or a very "with-it" dress. She has obviously never been given a present like this before

I told them in the shop you weren't exactly . . . or exactly . . . either. I got it from that little shop by the tube station. What's it called?

Louise "Girlomania."

George Yes. Is it all right?

Louise It's beautiful.
George It's—er—"with it", is it?
Louise Fantastic!
George I didn't choose it myself. The girl told me it's what they're wearing now. You really like it?
Louise It's amazing. Whoopee!

Louise unable to contain herself lets out a loud scream. With George trying to quieten her she rushes into the bedroom

George Don't wake the . . .

But Louise has gone

George smiles to himself; he is very pleased. He thinks for a moment, and then crosses to the window R and draws the curtains. The stage is in semi-darkness. He goes and selects a record of Perry Como, then turns on the desk lamp. He goes to the radiogram, opens it, and turns on the lamp on the drinks table. He starts the record and then picks up the flowers from the drinks table and puts them into a whisky glass. After a moment's hesitation he puts a spot of soda-water into the glass and puts it on the table L of the settee. He then goes into the kitchen, taking off his jacket and putting it on the back of a chair. He turns off the kitchen light and takes his apron from its hook by the door. He fetches the cake to the top of the refrigerator and puts the bottle of wine in the door of the refrigerator. He selects a grapefruit and puts it into the fruit basket. As he does so the doorbell rings. He stops, consults his watch, and stops the record. Still carrying the fruit, he goes to the front door, turns on the remaining lounge lights, and opens the door

Davey is standing there in gay party clothes

George's attitude towards Davey is now easier and more confident

George Hi, man.
Davey (*non-plussed*) Hi.

There is a pause

George Well man! We haven't seen much of you in our pad lately, man.
Davey Like I say, man, not my scene.
George Oh I don't know, man. We'd be delighted for you to pop down to our pad any time, man. Real cool, man.
Davey (*frowning*) Yeah. How're mummy freak and baby freak?
George Fab. Freaking out fine!
Davey (*seeing the tug-boat toy*) Hey, dig the little tug-boat, man.
George Yes. It's called a tuggy-tooter.

They play with it briefly

Is there anything else I can show you?
Davey No thanks.

George Anything I can do to help?
Davey Nope. (*He sits on the settee*)
George I dig-dug-digged—the guitar music earlier on.
Davey Mm.
George Yep. Smooth. He's new isn't he?
Davey He is a she.
George Ah yes.
Davey A real raver. Oh, man!

Davey laughs. George joins in

   You know what I mean?
George (*stopping laughing*) No, I'm afraid I don't.

   Louise enters

Louise George, it fits beautifully. (*She sees Davey*) (*Awkwardly*) Hi.
Davey Hi, Mummy chick. A real slim Mummy chick.
Louise Well—nearly back to normal.
Davey Great. Far out. (*To George*) A generous daddy.
George Well, after all it's only "bread", man.

Louise shoots George a glance

Louise What do you want, Davey?
Davey I come to tell you of a happy musical happening upstairs tonight.
Louise Lucky you got your record-player repaired.
Davey Music, dancing and spaghetti for all.
George Spaghetti for all! Sounds a really raving scene, man.
Davey (*to Louise*) It'll be really groovy. Nice sounds. Smooth dancing.
   Why don't you guys join us?
George Er—well, that's decent of you, but—er . . .
Louise (*cutting in*) We've got baby sitting problems.
George Yes.
Davey Oh. (*Moving to her*) Maybe one of you could come.
Louise Not me.
George And I don't imagine you'd want me to . . .

Davey silences him with a glare

Davey (*to Louise*) Would have been pleasant. We sort of miss you. *I* sort
   of miss you.
Louise (*quietly*) Thanks all the same.
Davey O.K. Keep happy. (*To George*) See you, Dad.
George See you, Kid.

   Davey gives him a withering look and exits

Louise (*to George*) Why'd you have to make such a fool of yourself?
   (*Imitating him*) See you, Kid!
George (*after a pause*) I'll start dinner.

George moves to the kitchen as Louise lights her cigarette. George stops

Are you sure you wouldn't like to go upstairs?

Louise (*a little too strongly*) Of course I'm sure.

George I wouldn't mind, honestly. It might do you good.

Louise I said I didn't want to go! Bunch of kids. (*She points to the grape-fruit*) If you stand there any longer with that thing it'll go mouldy.

George goes into the kitchen and starts to lay the table. Louise goes up to the front door and stands there thoughtfully. After a moment she pulls herself together and comes cheerfully into the kitchen

Do you know what I feel like right now?

George No.

George, during the ensuing dialogue, puts the two steaks under the grill with a pat of butter on each

Louise (*not unpleasantly*) Like we're an old married couple.

George (*returning to laying the table*) Silly.

Louise An old married couple taking the night off from their seven kids.

George Seven?

Louise A *young* old married couple, of course.

George A half young, half old married couple.

Louise You're not all that old, are you?

George Good Lord no! I'm thirty-nine.

Louise Bloody hell!

George looks up

My father's thirty-nine.

George I'm surprised the poor old fellow's got enough strength left to have it off with the neighbour.

Louise Bloody hell, though, thirty-nine.

George I think the sooner we get you into Parliament the better. You can vote us the old age pension at forty.

George has now finished the steaks and starts to cut one of the grapefruits in half

Louise (*after a pause*) Hell, though, thirty-nine.

George glares at her

George How old did you think I was, for heaven's sake?

Louise I don't know. Sort of early thirties.

George Well I'll take that as a compliment. Sit down, will you? Mind your new dress.

Louise sits

Louise (*quietly*) Bloody hell. Thirty-nine.

George glares at her

George Do you want sugar with your grapefruit?

Louise No, thanks.

George Here you are. One grapefruit à la fussy-arse. (*He puts the grape-fruit in front of her*)

Louise I wish you wouldn't use language like that, George.

George (*almost laughing at her effrontery*) Oh!

Louise It doesn't sound nice coming from you.

George puts his own grapefruit on the table

George All right. I'll moderate my language in future.

Louise Aren't *you* going to sit down?

George Yes. It just takes longer for we old folk to manage it. (*He puts on his jacket and sits*) I suppose I must seem pretty ancient to you.

Louise I feel pretty ancient myself lately.

George You certainly don't look it tonight.

Louise That's good. How do I look?

George Well sort of . . .

Louise Sexy?

George (*awkwardly*) Beautiful.

They are both suddenly self-conscious

Let's eat our grapefruit.

Louise (*with gentle irony*) Are we on a time schedule then?

George I just don't want to overcook the steak. I want you to really enjoy your dinner.

Louise I'll enjoy it, honest.

George I want everything to be perfect.

Louise Would you like me to sign something? All right, take it easy.

George All right. (*Sitting back*) We'll just relax—take our time. (*Rising*) I'd better turn the steak over. How do you like yours?

Louise I don't mind.

George Well done?

Louise I don't mind.

George Medium.

Louise (*louder*) I don't mind.

George Bloody?

Louise I don't bloody mind!

George turns the steaks

George Medium. That's the safest, isn't it?

Louise I'm sure it is.

George (*sitting*) There we are. (*Rising suddenly*) Here I'm forgetting.

Louise You'll give me indigestion.

George goes to get the glasses

What are they for?

George Champagne.

Louise Champagne?

George We're celebrating. The baby. (*He starts opening the champagne*)

Louise Are we going to celebrate like this *every* ten days?

George No! Actually it's not only baby.

Louise What else?

George My emancipation.

Louise What exactly does that mean?

George It means the look on Mr Saunders' face when I said I was going out to buy nappies and a potty. (*By now he has opened the champagne and is pouring*)

Louise (*after a thoughtful pause*) Don't pin too much faith on me, George. Me and the baby.

George stops pouring the champagne. He does not know what to say. He then pulls himself together and hands her a glass of champagne

George There we are! Let's drink to—your son.

Louise Here's to him.

They drink

George Don't you think you ought to give him a name fairly soon?

Louise I think I'll wait and see what he turns out like first. You know whether he's going to be a Peregrine or a Charlie. (*Referring to champagne*) This isn't bad is it? Can I have some more.

George You'd better not have too much. It'll affect the baby.

Louise Will it?

George Of course.

Louise You mean he'll get a sort of champagne milk shake?

George Something like that. (*He pours a little in her glass*)

Louise Top it up. It might help to knock him out.

George All right, just a drop then!

She tips the bottle, filling her glass. George starts to chuckle

Louise What are you laughing at?

George It's nothing.

Louise Come on.

George No, it's nothing.

Louise (*warningly*) George.

George Well, all this chat about feeding the baby—(*he chuckles again*)— reminds me of one of the first rude jokes I ever heard.

Louise (*interested*) Do you know rude jokes?

George No, I don't. I just remembered this one, that's all. It's rather silly.

Louise Go on then.

George No.

Louise Go on.

George Well. There's this little boy, you see. About five years old. Maybe he was a bit older. I don't think it matters. He was probably six or seven.

Louise Get on with it.

George Well, this little boy was watching his mother feed the baby—you know his little brother—or was it his sister? I don't think it makes any difference whether the baby's a boy or girl. Anyway, the little boy is watching the mother feed the baby. Not at the bottle, I mean, feeding the baby at her—you know.

Louise (*patiently*) I know. Yes.

George So the little boy said, "Mummy, what can baby drink?" She said, "Milk and orange juice". So he said, "Which one's orange juice?"

George chuckles merrily. Louise manages a polite smile

(*Stopping laughing*) I'm sorry. It's a bit rude, isn't it?

Louise (*sarcastically*) Filthy.

George I don't really like dirty stories. Hang on a second. (*He rises*)

Louise Are you off again?

George gets the flowers from the side settee table

George What's the grapefruit like?

Louise Grapefruit.

George (*sitting*) Right. (*Rising*) Oh!

Louise You're like a jack-in-the-box!

George hurries into the lounge and switches the record-player on. He starts the record again from the beginning

George Perry Como.

George watches the record and awaits for the first sound to come through so that he can adjust the volume. The music comes out quite loudly. Louise looks in disbelief in the direction of the music and rolls her eyes to heaven. George lowers the volume

Louise (*calling*) How did you know Perry Como turns me on?

George Does he really? Is that quiet enough?

Louise No!

George lowers the volume even more, then goes back into the kitchen and returns to his grapefruit

You're stopping now are you?

George Ooo! Steaks! Look I don't want to rush you, but if you're through with your grapefruit . . .

Louise gulps down a quick spoonful

Louise I'm through. Can I help!

George No.

George takes the grapefruit, puts them on the side and goes to the stove. During the ensuing dialogue George puts the steaks on plates and brings them to the table. He then goes to the refrigerator and returns with a bowl of salad

Louise You really like to cook don't you?

George Yes. What do *you* like to do?

Louise (*surprised*) Do?

George Mm. What would you say you really enjoy doing? I mean what do you want to do most in the whole wide world?

Louise Hell, when you put it like that—I don't know. Do we all have to *do* something?

George Well it's—er—usual.

Louise I'm just trying to *understand* things.

George You can't go through life doing nothing but try to understand things.

Louise Why not?

George There's more to life than that.

Louise You mean like bridge parties once a month and dinner with Helen every Wednesday?

George (*trying to keep it gay*) There's other things.

Louise Sure. Musical evenings with Perry Como.

George When you're older . . .

Louise (*furiously cutting in*) Don't give me that crap!

George (*pacifying her*) All right. All right.

Louise That's what people always say. Hell, it makes me angry when people say that.

George (*jokingly*) I'll just move the champagne in case you feel like throwing things. (*He does so*) Now, there's the salad. Help yourself. I put tarragon in this dressing.

She sits rigid

Don't let your steak get cold.

Louise (*sullenly*) I like cold steak.

George realizes that he cannot cope

George I don't know what to say half the time, that's all.

Louise Then don't say it.

Guitar music is heard from above followed by a couple of shouts. Louise looks upwards and George glances at her

My back's aching a bit. I think I'll sit on the sofa. (*She gets up and moves into the lounge, switching off the record as she goes*)

George What about your steak?

Louise I'm not hungry any more.

George just nods blankly. She sits on the settee

George You see—your whole experience is so different from mine. When I was your age——

Louise Here we go again!

George —I didn't question things very much. You went to school, you got a job, you got married. (*Smiling*) You got old at thirty-nine—and there it was.

Louise Maybe that's enough for you.

George (*shrugging*) That's how it was.

Louise Well things are different now, old chum.

She picks up a magazine and starts to read it. There is a slight pause

George (*curtly*) I think I'll take my coat off.

Louise Why don't you go all out and loosen your tie?

George All right, I will. (*He takes his jacket off and then notices that the record is not playing*) What happened to my music? Did it go off?

Louise I turned it off.

George Why?

Louise shoots him a glance

(*Angrily*) I see! (*He pours his glass full of champagne*) Did it have some semblance of melody. Was that the trouble?

She does not answer, so he knocks back the champagne in one gulp. He fills his glass again

I chose that record specially.

She still does not answer, so he drinks the champagne

I thought it was very nice dinner music.

Louise (*looking up*) Are you Perry Como's mother or something?

There is a bump from the flat above followed by a loud yell and lots of raucous laughter. Louise looks upwards. George fills his glass and drinks

George You'd much rather be up there with them, wouldn't you?

She does not answer

Wouldn't you?

Still no reply

Well, go on. (*He opens the flat door*) You haven't eaten enough here to spoil your appetite. They'll have yards of spaghetti left. It must be better than being cooped up in the old curiosity shop with old fussy-arse. This isn't exactly "your own thing", is it? You must be bored stiff.

Louise throws down the magazine

Louise You're right, I am bored stiff. Bored bloody stiff!

George (*pleased*) Now we're getting somewhere. (*He fills his glass*)

Louise In fact if it wasn't for those entertaining phone calls you have from your sister every day life would be unbearable.

George Ah! My sister upsets you as well, does she?

Louise No, I love her. The latest news bulletin on her bladder inflammation. How many times she's been to the "loo" that day. She brightens up my life fantastically.

George You're right about Helen. She's foolish. She's unreasonable. God, she is a bore! But—she's my sister. And I can remember her when she wasn't foolish. When she wasn't unreasonable and when she wasn't a bore.

Louise She's been all those things since she was two and a half weeks old.

George And if I can make her life a little less intolerable with such a small sacrifice on my part, why shouldn't I? When you're older . . .

Louise Oh, bloody hell!

She rises and starts to move, but he grabs her arm

George When you're bloody older! You stop looking so hard for "Happiness" and settle for that which is "Tolerable". And all I do is try to make her life tolerable.

Louise You're hurting my arm.

George releases her arm

George You see, I'm old-fashioned enough to still believe in things like loyalty and consideration and that repulsive word—responsibility. I think I'll have another drink. (*He goes to fill his glass but the bottle is empty*)

Louise Don't you think you've had enough champagne?

George Definitely. I'll start on the whisky now.

Louise You'll be sick.

George Don't be an old fussy-arse! (*He moves to the drinks*)

A Hippy Boy hurries in with a guitar

Boy (*to Louise*) Hey, where's the scene, man?

George What the hell do you want?

The boy turns and sees George

Boy Oh. I'm sorry. I'm looking for Davey's pad.

George Ah, Davey's pad!

Boy Hey! Are you Davey?

George Davey's got the pad above, man.

Boy What?

George Davey's got the pad above.

Louise It's upstairs.

Boy Oh.

George And it's all happening up there tonight, kiddy baby.

Boy (*eyeing George*) Yeah. That's the story, man.

George That's the story, that's the story! Smooth dancing. Nice sounds. And enough spaghetti to knit you a string vest.

Boy (*blankly*) Yeah. Well, see you upstairs.

A Hippy Girl, happily high, dances her way into the room

George Could be, man. See you. Don't forget to take Salome with you.

The Hippy Boy and Girl exit

George closes the door

It's all happening up there tonight, kiddy baby. Yes, it's going to be real cool up there tonight, Mummy chick. Don't know how you can keep yourself away. Now, where was I? Ah, yes! (*He pours himself a large whisky*)

Louise You're in a crazy mood.

George I know. Maybe I am crazy. (*He pulls a "crazy" face*) I'm in a "let's ask questions we've never asked before" mood. For instance. What was in your mind when you were "having it off" with "juicy chops" eighteen-year-old Daddy"?

Louise What sort of bloody question is that?

George A pretty bloody good one. The first thing you ought to try and understand is yourself. If you didn't intend to have a baby I'm sure a modern girl like you would have taken precautions.

Louise All right. So *what*?

George So you *wanted* to have a baby. For whatever daft reason—to spite your parents—to be an instant grown-up, or for the sheer novelty of it —you *wanted* that baby.

Louise O.K. I wanted it. Now are you satisfied?

George Right. You decided to bring another life into this world and you're *responsible* for that little thing—whether he's a Peregrine, a Charlie or a Nancy! You're trapped all right and you trapped yourself, kid.

Louise And you're smacking your lips over it. You're so damned dull, you'd like to make everyone else dull. You don't know how to live. You and your sister are a right pair. A couple of old maids.

This remark hits home on George. He moves away

George (*trying to be gay*) It's been a super dinner party hasn't it? Yes, quite a celebration. (*He toasts the bedroom*) Happy Birthday, little basket! (*He drinks. Flatly*) It's a pity about tonight.

Louise Yes. You went to a lot of trouble.

George "Passed" on effort. "Failed" on entertainment. (*He sits on the settee*)

Louise Bloody hell! Don't always be so apologetic. It's my fault. Hit me or something!

George Don't be so ridiculous.

Louise Well, do *something*, for God's sake.

George I am doing something.

Louise What?

George Getting drunk.

Louise Let's hope that puts a bit of life into you. Maybe *then* you'll hit me.

George I doubt it.

Louise What *will* you do—rip my clothes off, jump on top of me and make mad passionate love to me?

George gives her a nervous look and "downs" his whisky

After you'd said "excuse me", of course.

There is a pause as she surveys him. The "anger" game is now finished for her and the "sex" game is on

When I woke up this morning I felt decidedly fruity.

George looks around uneasily and his eyes fall on the steaks

George Pity about those steaks.

Louise Shows I'm getting back to normal. It's funny how you feel sexy in the morning, isn't it?

George I—er—well, I—er—I suppose one feels relaxed after a good night's sleep.

Louise Oh, you're the same in the morning, are you?

George No.

Louise Prefer it in the evening.

George No—er . . .

Louise Afternoon?

George Look, I don't really . . .

Louise Not fussy what time, eh, George? (*She sits close to him*) I thought you were going to loosen your tie? (*She starts to remove his tie*)

George Louise, please—our relationship is dodgy enough without complicating it further.

Louise Complicating it?

George With sex.

Louise Teaser! (*She is now undoing his shirt buttons*)

George I thought you were going upstairs.

Louise That was your idea, not mine.

George Can I get you a whisky?

Louise No.

George Do you mind if I have one.

Louise Yes.

He gets up with his shirt flapping and goes to the drinks cupboard. Louise follows him and starts to untuck his shirt as he pours his whisky

George Louise, please leave my shirt alone.

Louise Much nicer without your shirt on.

He moves away from her. The movement neatly leaves Louise holding his shirt. George sits hurriedly on the settee with his drink. Louise sits next to him and feels his shoulder

That's better, isn't it?

George It's a bit nippy, actually.

Louise (*suddenly*) Here, George.

George Yes?

Louise When did you last have it off?

George We really should have eaten our steaks, you know.

Louise George, I'm talking to you.

George Over a pound a pound.

Louise When did you last have it off?

George And that was from Sainsbury's, too.

In answer George downs his drink

Louise (*gently*) You poor old bugger.

George What's that supposed to mean?

Louise You haven't been getting your rations lately, have you?

George gets up and hurries over to pour himself another drink

Right, lad! You said you wanted a celebration tonight and you're going to get it.

George (*backing away*) I want to finish my drink.

Louise You've had more than enough, already. (*She starts to undo his trousers*)

George Louise! Stop that! Behave yourself! The baby's in there.

Louise Fast asleep.

George He might come in!

Louise Don't be daft.

George's trousers drop to his ankles

My God, you're sexy! (*She starts to take his shoes off*)

George Louise, I don't want to do it.

Louise Neither do I, darling. I'm forcing myself.

George No, I really don't. Can't you understand?

Louise I can understand you've got yourself all twisted up about it and I'm going to fix it. (*She pulls his trousers off*)

George I don't want it fixed.

Louise You do. (*She starts taking his socks off*)

George I don't. I don't want to do it, I tell you.

Louise Well, I do, so shut up! (*She has got his socks off*)

George (*getting up*) No!

Louise (*exasperated*) Bloody hell!

George (*angrily*) I'm sorry!

Louise A girl can only go so far, you know. The fellow's got to help a bit.

George I don't want to help. For heaven's sake listen to what I'm saying.

Louise Just now you said I was beautiful.

George doesn't answer

I see! You don't fancy me. Come on. Let's lay it on the line, George. I mean, I've practically offered it to you on a plate, haven't I? You don't want me, do you? Do you?!

George (*shouting*) *No*, I don't. I want to be left in peace.

Louise (*shouting*) Well, that can be arranged, chum. (*She moves to door, but stops*) If you don't think I'm sexy there's someone upstairs who does.

George Don't you ever think about anything else?!

Louise Don't you ever think about it at all?!

There is a pause as they look at each other. The door bell rings. George freezes

George (*horrified*) Who on earth can that be?!

Louise Probably your sister.

George Oh my God! (*He quickly puts his trousers on not noticing that they are now inside out*)
Louise (*calling out*) Who is it?
Davey (*off*) Davey.
Louise (*moving to door*) Coming.
George No!

Davey enters, and stops on seeing George trying to zip up his "flies".

It takes George a few seconds to realize why he cannot find the zip, during which time a broad grin spreads across Davey's face

Finally George collects his clothes and exits into the bedroom

Davey Dad having a little streak, was he?
Louise What do you want, Davey?
Davey See if you care to change your mind.

Louise does not answer

Louise (*flatly*) What about?

Davey gives her a pleasant grin for an answer

Davey (*after a pause*) Haven't you had enough of it down here?
Louise Would you like to rephrase that question?
Davey (*after a pause*) I'd like you back upstairs permanent—know what I mean?
Louise (*flatly*) No.
Davey (*taken aback*) Well, you know . . .
Louise (*after a pause*) No, I don't know, Davey. Tell me. (*She just looks at him, still not helping*)
Davey We got it together, you and me. I mean—I've got no chick. (*He hesitates, then starts to go*)
Louise Davey!

Davey stops

(*Kindly*) Thanks.
Davey Yeah. See you.

Davey exits. George enters from the bedroom

Louise George.
George Oh. I heard the door shut. I thought you'd gone upstairs. Why haven't you gone?
Louise George . . .
George (*pressing on*) Davey's waiting, off you go!
Louise (*levelly*) Do you want to make love to me tonight?
George Davey will be waiting.
Louise Or any other night?

George does not answer

    Louise goes out of the front door, closing it

George moves towards the front door. He hesitates, then opens it. From upstairs comes the sound of a cheer and some laughter. He closes the door. He takes off the Como record and looks at it. He closes his eyes, near to tears. Suddenly he smashes the record to pieces against the table. From the bedroom the baby starts to cry

George Oh, shut your fussy-arse row!

    George hurries into the bedroom with the cry getting louder

The telephone rings

    After a moment George comes out of the bedroom with the baby over his shoulder, patting its back

(*To the baby*) There, there. Daddy knows. (*He picks up the telephone and speaks into it*) Hullo, Helen . . . Oh dear, I'm sorry to hear that . . . That sounds nasty . . . No, I've got time for a chat, yes . . . Oh dear . . . Oh dear . . . Oh dear . . .

He picks up a baby's toy and is trying to make the baby smile, as—

the CURTAIN *falls*

SCENE 2

The same. The following morning

The sun is shining through the windows. George, dressed for the office, is hanging out the nappies on the line. The front door opens and Louise enters, still wearing the dress she had on the previous evening. She looks very bedraggled and obviously has had no sleep. With her eyes barely open she walks down to the settee and sits there almost asleep

George (*after a pause*) Would you like a cup of tea?
Louise (*mumbling*) Yes, please.

George pours her a cup of tea and takes it through

George I'll be leaving for the office in five minutes. You can help yourself to egg and bacon then.
Louise (*horrified at the thought of it*) Give over! Baby all right?
George Fine. He's fast asleep at the moment.
Louise (*surprised*) Is he? That's good!
George Took me quite a lot of time to get him off though. Wouldn't go

to sleep. I fed him twice, bathed him twice and changed his nappy at least eleven times. (*He returns to the kitchen where he proceeds to sterilize the bottles with Milton*)

Louise What the hell for?

George I got the impression that's what he wanted. He kept on crying.

Louise You should have just turned him over.

George I never thought of that.

Louise Keeping the poor little thing up all night.

George shoots her a glance at this remark

No wonder he's fast asleep.

There is a pause

I had a fantastic time at the party.

George Jolly good.

Louise Fantastic! It's only just broken up. What time is it, by the way?

George Six and three-quarter minutes past nine.

Louise Whoopee! What a night.

George Yes, I must say for a "quiet" party, you certainly shook the ceiling a bit. The record-player, the guitar and all that.

Louise How about the bongo drums?

George Yes. They came through quite clearly. The baby seemed to prefer the guitar actually.

Louise (*chuckling*) Yes, it was wild. I'd forgotten how crazy it gets when you're on dope.

George Louise, you didn't . . .

Louise Why not? That was much later, of course. After the booze. What the hell? An orgy's not much fun till the dope gets going.

George Well—as long as you had a pleasant evening.

Louise Like I said—fantastic.

There is a pause

Louise I'm leaving, George. Me and the baby.

George just nods

George When?

Louise Today. This morning. Soon as I can get ready.

George I'm glad you two made it up.

Louise Which two?

George You and Davey. Youth calls to youth, all that sort of thing. He's got a lot in his favour.

Louise I'm not going back to Davey.

George (*surprised*) Where *are* you going then, Bradford?

Louise No fear.

George Then, where?

Louise Haven't the faintest idea.

George Louise, for heaven's sake . . .

Louise I'm getting changed and then we're leaving.

Louise hurries into the bedroom

George (*following her to the door*) Louise, don't be so damn . . .

The door is closed in his face. He hesitates a moment and then goes to the phone. He dials a number and waits for it to answer

George (*on the phone*) Supervisor, please . . . Ah, good morning, Mr Saunders. It's Mr Clarke here. I'd like the morning off please, sir . . . A domestic crisis . . . A Personal Problem . . . It can come off my annual leave, can't it, sir . . . (*Getting angry*) Well, I'll do my best to get in by twelve, but . . . I realize that, Mr Saunders, but it's the first time in eighteen years that I've asked for a morning off . . . Well, of course it's short notice, so was my Personal Problem . . . (*Firmly*) Mr Saunders, I am taking the morning off, I will get in as soon as possible, and if you don't like it I'm here to say you are a crappy pissy-arse! (*He puts the phone down angrily, takes off his jacket and loosens his tie*)

Louise comes out of the bedroom, having changed, with a large pile of baby clothes. She proceeds to put these in the pram and then goes round the room collecting up the toys which she also puts in the pram

Louise You're going to be late for work.
George I'm not going in this morning.
Louise (*surprised*) Why not?
George I don't feel like it.
Louise You'll cop it from your supervisor.
George I've just dealt with Mr Saunders, thank you very much.
Louise Here, there's hope for you yet.
George Louise, please stay. At least until the baby's a little stronger.
Louise No!
George All right, all right. There's only one way out of this. You stay here. I'll move out. (*He marches towards the bedroom*)
Louise Don't be daft.
George (*stopping*) You should be able to stick it for a few weeks if old phony establishment fussy-arse moves out.

George goes into the bedroom

Louise (*yelling*) I'm the one who's going.
George (*off*) It's the perfect solution.
Louise (*yelling*) You can stuff your sacrifices. Give it to the Save the Children Fund.

George returns with a pile of suits, shirts, handkerchiefs, socks, etc.

George With me out of the way, you'll have a ball. You can sit around all day trying to understand everything. (*He puts his clothes down on the settee and gets a case from the corner of the room*)

Louise I'm going. You're staying.

George (*ignoring this*) And in the evening Davey and the bongo drummer can baby sit for you. (*He throws his stuff into his case*)

Louise And where the hell do you think you'll go?

George I shall go to Helen's.

Louise God help us all.

George She'll make me very welcome.

Louise Not half. Once you set up home with your sister, she'll never let go of you.

George (*angrily*) Listen, I'm not doing this for you, remember. I'm thinking of him. (*He points to the bedroom*) And it's about time you started thinking about him for a change. When are you going to grow up?

Louise I *am* grown up.

George (*shouting*) Then act like it. You selfish hippy.

She slaps his face. He is shattered for a moment but controls himself

(*On his dignity*) I shall get my sponge bag.

George marches into the bedroom

The phone rings. She lifts the receiver

Louise (*on the phone*) Hullo, how're your varicose veins this morning? . . . Oh, good morning Mr Saunders . . . Yes. Hang on a second. (*She calls quietly into bedroom*) George!

George enters with his sponge bag

George What is it?

Louise It's your Mr Saunders.

George Oh.

She hands him the telephone. During the speech his "bravado" deserts him

George (*on the phone; firmly*) Clarke, here . . . I beg your pardon, sir? . . . Oh. I didn't think I'd slammed the phone down. I thought our conversation was finished, so I replaced my receiver . . . Repeat what, sir? . . . The last thing I said. Er—well, I can't quite recall . . . Oh, *you* can —crappy pissy-arse . . . What a quaint phrase . . . No, sir. But I'm sure you must be mistaken though. Yes. (*Chuckling pleasantly*) What I said was "Happy Christ-y-marse" . . . Yes . . . Yes . . . And a happy New Year to you, too, sir. (*He puts the phone down*)

Louise I liked the way you dealt with your Mr Saunders.

George Yes. Well—(*tamely*) there you are. (*Suddenly business-like*) I'll pick up the rest of my things some other time.

Louise I am the one who's going.

George Perhaps you'll be good enough to forward my letters.

Louise *I won't be here.*

George Helen's phone number and address are in this book.

He hands her the address book which she rips in two. She moves off and collects the nappies off the line, which she throws into the pram

Now, money.
Louise I don't want your money.

George writes out a cheque

Louise exits to the bedroom

George You're not used to housekeeping, are you? Well, it doesn't go far I can tell you that. Especially with old Juicy Chops around the place.

Louise returns with some clothes

George holds out the cheque

Here's ten pounds.
Louise I don't want your money.
George There you are. I think you'll find you can cash it at the sweet shop.

She takes the cheque, tears it up and throws the pieces into the air

You may as well keep the newspapers coming. And the *Radio Times*.

During the ensuing dialogue George unpacks her pram and re-hangs the nappies while Louise unpacks his suitcase by throwing his clothes all over the room

Louise I don't give a bugger about your newspapers 'cos I won't be here! And you can just unpack your suitcase because you're stopping and I'm going. Get it into your thick head that I'm leaving, walking out, doing my own thing! (*She sees George re-hanging the nappies*) And leave my things alone. (*She goes up behind him and removes the line. She puts the nappies back in her pram*)
George Now you may find the "fridge" needs a bit of defrost.
Louise (*yelling*) Defrost it yourself!
George Help yourself to anything you might require. (*He opens the refrigerator*) There are plenty of bits and pieces in here. Oh, and you might finish up the baby's birthday cake. (*He transfers the cake from the top of the refrigerator to the oak chest*) And I made a spare feed for you, just in case. (*He fetches the spare feed and puts it beside the cake*)
Louise (*nearly crying with anger*) Listen to me, will you?! I'm going. Walking out. Me and the baby. For good.

During his ensuing speech she sees the cake, picks it up and takes her arm back to hit him with it

George (*collecting his clothes and throwing them into his case*) I'll ring you every evening to see how you're going. And if there are any problems with the baby or yourself don't hesitate to phone me at the office during the day or Helen's during the evening. Good-bye, and thank you. (*He* *takes the cake from her uplifted arm*) No, I think I should keep that in the fridge in case the cream goes off.

They look at each other for a moment. Louise snatches George's bowler hat and pushes the crown in. He grabs it and crams it on his head. Suddenly he smacks her across the face. She is astonished

Louise You do that again.

George does so. She slaps him. He slaps her. She goes to slap him but stops and bursts into tears, collapsing on to the settee

> *George picks up his case, hat and umbrella, looks at her, hesitates and then goes out, closing the door. The door immediately opens again and George re-enters*

George And crying won't get you anywhere.

> *George moves out of the front door and returns again*

I've put up with all I'm going to from you. I used to have a nice orderly smooth life. You come in and in ten days I'm ready for the psychiatrist.

He bangs his hat against the door. Louise sobs even louder

(*Stopping*) Go on . . . Cry! Drown yourself. (*He bangs his umbrella on table and the handle flies off*) I just don't understand you. I've tried. God knows I've tried. Something must be the matter with you.
Louise (*wailing*) I'm Gemini.
George You're what?
Louise Gemini.

George starts throwing her clothes over the room and inadvertently the nappies land on the light fitting

George There must be millions of bloody pissy-arse Gemini but they don't carry on like you do. And stop that crying because it doesn't affect me at all.

She carries on sobbing

You can cry as much as you like. (*Gently*) Louise, please stop crying.

He goes to her and puts his hand on her shoulder. This makes her cry even more

(*Angrily*) What's the matter? You're not crying just because you're Gemini, are you?

She shakes her head. George sits on the settee a little distance from her. Finally her sobs stop

Louise (*sniffing*) I must look a sight.
George You do, rather.

Louise sobs again. George puts his head in his hands. He inadvertently starts up one of the mechanical toys. This makes Louise look up. She smiles through her tears. George grins back at her.

    Now what was all that about?
Louise (*flatly*) I had a lousy time last night.
George Last night?
Louise At the party.

George tries to take this in

George But you said . . .
Louise (*cutting in*) I know!
George Well—why did you have a lousy time.

Louise sniffs

Louise Have you got a hanky?

George finds his handkerchief and gives it to her. She blows her nose loudly and hands it back to him.

George I thought you had a lot of fun. You stayed out late enough.
Louise I know. I did that on purpose.
George What for?
Louise So you'd *think* I had a lot of fun, you fool.
George (*confused*) I don't know.
Louise Everybody else was having a good time.
George Wasn't any of what you said true? About the pot-smoking and the orgy?
Louise No, they were just kids having a good time. I could hardly keep my eyes open. I nearly fell asleep twice. In the end I went and had a kip in the bus shelter. I kept wishing I was home.
George Haven't I said all along you should go back to Bradford.
Louise No. Home.

George realizes what she means

George I see.
Louise Well, it's the only home I've got. It's where the baby is. (*Still angry at herself*) I should've been having a good time but I couldn't. I kept wondering if you were choking the baby with that bloody bottle of yours.
George No problems there at all.
Louise Hell, I've got problems. "Me" problems. I don't know who I am or where I'm at.
George For heaven's sake, most people go through the whole of life not knowing what it's all about.
Louise I can't wait that long. I'll tell you one thing I know. I'm a phony.

George looks at her

    Yes, I am. I am. A lousy phony. I'm not really anything. I thought I wanted to—I don't know. Do me own thing. Drop out. But I hadn't got the guts. The kids who do that know how they want to live and they live that way twenty-four hours a day. Me? I was a half-arse drop out. Now, I'm a half-arse mother. I'm a half-arse everything. God, I'm a phony. Knowing me I'll probably turn out to be a half-arse phony.

George tries to think of something comforting to say

George (*cheerfully*) Well—half an arse is better than . . .

Louise, not listening to George, gets up and walks about to calm herself

You're so hard on yourself. You want everything *now*.

There is a pause as each tries to think

Louise George.
George Yes?
Louise Don't go to Helen's.
George It's where I belong, isn't it? Two old maids together.
Louise Please stay here.
George With you?

Louise nods

It'll be absolutely awful won't it? Nothing but arguments. I don't think my jaw could stand it.
Louise I'm sorry.
George And what about my fussing and nagging? It's as important to me, as a damn good punch up is to you . . .
Louise You still don't understand about your fussing and nagging, do you? I *like* it.
George You've got a funny way of showing it.
Louise (*moving behind the settee*) Gemini.
George Gemini's got an awful lot to answer for!
Louise When you're nagging me or fussing at me it makes me feel secure. As though somebody really cared. (*She puts her arms round his neck*)
George You said something yesterday. You said, "Don't pin too much faith on me".
Louise Yes.
George Well—you mustn't pin too much faith on me either.
Louise I won't.

She takes his face in her hands and kisses him gently on the lips

(*Quietly*) That's the first kiss we've had.

George can only nod

If you're stopping why don't you put your suitcase away.

George nods thoughtfully, gets up and moves towards the bedroom

Don't wake the baby.

George goes into the bedroom

Louise looks pleased with herself and sits on the settee

   George returns

George He's sound asleep, bless him.

Louise George!

George Yes? What is it?

Louise I've just thought of something. I know what I'm going to call the baby.

George What?

Louise (*proudly*) George.

George (*pleased*) Don't be silly.

Louise You're almost the father. We practically had the baby together, didn't we? Have you got another Christian name?

George Yes.

Louise What?

George Humphrey.

Louise Well, he doesn't have to have two Christian names, does he?

The telephone rings. George lifts the receiver

George (*on the phone*) Two-three-nine-oh . . . Hullo, Helen . . . No, I didn't go in this morning. Look, I'm rather tied up at the moment. I'll see you on Wednesday then for dinner . . . Your place, yes. Oh Helen —I'll be bringing Louise with me . . . Yes, but we can arrange a baby sitter. Actually we've got some jolly nice chums upstairs . . . No, I'm sure she'd love to come.

Louise pulls a ghastly face

   She's nodding and saying "yes please" . . . (*Firmly*) Helen, it'll be fine . . . Positive. Good night. (*He puts the receiver down*) How was that?

Louise (*smiling*) Quite masterful.

She puts the radio on and music is heard. She goes to him and puts her arm round his waist

   I haven't felt so relaxed for ages.

George It can't last, Louise.

Louise (*lightly*) No you're right—— Probably not.

George Sooner or later I'll say something and get the record-player wrapped round my head.

Louise starts to dance him towards the settee

Louise George, I'm ever so glad you took the morning off.

George (*apprehensively*) Mr Saunders expects me in by twelve.

Louise Fair enough. (*She starts to kiss his neck*)

George Louise, please . . .

She carries on caressing him

   Louise . . .

She kisses him, and after a moment he breaks it

Louise, I want you to . . .

She stops him talking by kissing him again. After a moment he starts to talk while still kissing

Mm—mm . . .

Louise (*breaking the kiss*) Don't speak with your mouth full.

Louise kisses him again, and after a moment he breaks it. She kisses him and eases him down on to the settee, as—

the CURTAIN *falls*

FURNITURE AND PROPERTY LIST

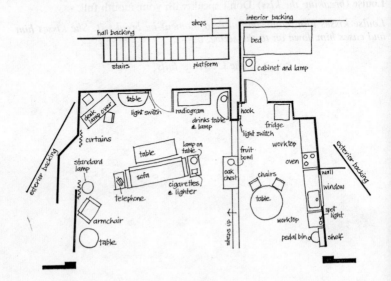

ACT I

On stage: **LOUNGE**
Occasional table. *On it*: ashtray, cigarette lighter
Armchair
Standard lamp
Desk. *On it:* writing materials, address book
Desk chair
Console table. *On it:* bowler hat
Shelf behind table. *On it:* records including Perry Como, telephone directories including Yellow Pages
Large put-u-up settee. *On it:* cushions. *In it:* mattress with fitted sheet
Table above settee. *On it:* magazine, ashtray
Table R of settee. *On it:* telephone, ashtray
Table L of settee. *On it*: table lamp, ashtray, "crumpet warmer" with 5 cigarettes, lighter
Radiogram. *On it:* ornate vase
Console table below radiogram. *On it*: table lamp, whisky, soda, glasses, other drinks
Oak chest. *On it:* bowl of fruit including real banana, china swan, ashtray
Window curtains

KITCHEN

Refrigerator. *In it:* bottle of milk, tea towels on suckers at side

Wall cupboard. *In it:* cocoa. *On it:* scribbling pad, pencil. *On hook:* milk pan

Floor cupboard. *On it:* electric kettle, chutney, teapot. *In drawer:* table mat, napkin

Over (practical). *On it:* plate and bowl (on grill), pan of cooked rice, pan of Suki Yaki, pan containing burnt mixture of flour, water and gravy browning. *On hooks over:* 5 china mugs

Sink unit. *On draining-board:* plate rack. *In sink:* plastic bowl with water. *On window-sill:* brushes, pan scrubber, washing-up liquid

Second floor cupboard. *On it:* kitchen timer, sink tidy with cloths, etc.

On floor: pedal bin

Shelf. *On it:* glasses, ornaments, 2 wine glasses

Kitchen table. *On it:* table mat, spoon, fork, napkin, chopsticks, glass of water, salt, pepper, teaspoon, scales, chopping board with par-boiled chopped carrot, cooking knife, cookery book, bowls of sugar, raw egg, beans and sliced banana

2 upright kitchen chairs

Window curtains

BEDROOM

Bed made up with loosely laid sheets, blankets and counterpane

Bedside cabinet. *On it:* table, alarm clock

Off stage: 2 £5 notes **(George)**

Pile of bedding, containing 3 pillows (1 in pillowcase), 2 pillowcases, 1 double-size sheet, 2 large blankets

Large pair of man's pyjamas **(George)**

Mop and bucket **(George)**

Personal: **Louise:** shoulder-bag

George: butcher's-type apron; wristwatch

Davey: cigarette

ACT II

SCENE 1

Strike: All bedding, pillows, etc.

Mop and bucket

Yellow Pages directory

Dirty glasses

Vase from radiogram

China swan

Everything from kitchen table

Pans and plates from sink

Pans from stove

Empty bowls from previous Act cooking on working-top

Electric kettle

Bowler hat
Bed from bedroom

Set: Suitcase and pram in window bay
Louise's bag on armchair
Magazines on floor
Tug-boat toy on settee table
Salad bowl (empty) and servers on oak chest
Assorted small toys on floor and furniture
Yale key on chair
Clean glasses on drinks table
Salad in plastic container in refrigerator
Tea towels in original place
George's apron on hook
3 clothes pegs on window-sill
On working surface: salt and pepper pots, bowl of sugar, glacé
    cherries in saucer, jar with salad dressing, 2 fruit plates, oven
    cloth, kitchen knife, grapefruit knife, serving slice. *In drawer
    underneath:* 2 knives, 2 forks, 2 teaspoons, tablecloth, 2 napkins
On stove: 2 dinner plates, grill-pan in position
Line between bedroom door and wall downstage, with 4 nappies, 2
    baby dresses, towelling jumpsuit, all without clothes pegs
Cot in bedroom, with "baby" and small chair

Off stage: All the following for **George**'s first entrance:
Bowler hat
Umbrella
Outsize toy panda
Fancy cake in caterer's box
Flowers in tissue
Carrier bag of groceries, including 2 steaks, 2 grapefruit
½-bottle of champagne in vintner's bag
Carrier containing feeding bottles, dried milk, baby foods
Carrier containing miniature spring balance, surveying tape
Carrier containing child's potty
Boutique carrier containing dress for Louise

Personal: **Davey:** 2 cigarettes

SCENE 2

Strike: Bits of broken record
George's tie
Magazines from settee to armchair
Whisky bottle, salad box, oven cloth
Dirty glasses
Everything from kitchen table, including cloth
Cake box
Grill pan

Set: Electric toy dog on floor near settee

On kitchen table: teapot with tea, milk jug, teacup, saucer, *Daily Telegraph*

On working-top: tray with Milton sterilizer kit, 1 filled feeding bottle, empty bottles, etc., cup, saucer

4 nappies, pegged in place, on line

Off stage: Nappy **(George)**
Pile of clothes including baby clothes **(Louise)**
Pile of clothes **(George)**
Sponge bag **(George)**
Second pile of clothes **(Louise)**

Personal: **George:** cheque-book, biro pen, handkerchief

LIGHTING PLOT

Property fittings required: standard lamp, hanging lamp, chandelier, 3 table lamps, kitchen pendant, wall-mounted kitchen spotlight
Interior. A flat. The same scene throughout

ACT I. Night

To open: Lounge lit only by street-lamp through half-closed curtains. Kitchen lights on

Cue 1	**George** switches lounge lights on	(Page 1)
	Bring up all lounge lights except standard lamp	
Cue 2	**George** switches on standard lamp	(Page 2)
	Bring up standard lamp	
Cue 3	**Louise** exits to bedroom	(Page 7)
	Bring up bedroom lamp	
Cue 4	**George** switches lights off	(Page 8)
	Return to opening lighting	
Cue 5	**Louise** switches lights on	(Page 10)
	Revert to Cue 2	
Cue 6	**George** enters from bedroom	(Page 12)
	Take out bedroom lamp	
Cue 7	**George** exits to bedroom	(Page 19)
	Bring up bedroom lamp	
Cue 8	**George** switches off kitchen lights	(Page 24)
	Take out kitchen lighting	
Cue 9	**George** switches on table lamp	(Page 24)
	Bring up table lamp L *of settee*	
Cue 10	**George** switches off lights	(Page 24)
	Take out all lights in lounge except standard lamp and table lamp	
Cue 11	**George** switches off standard lamp	(Page 25)
	Take out standard lamp	
Cue 12	**Louise** switches off table lamp	(Page 25)
	Take out table lamp L *of settee*	
Cue 13	**Louise** switches on table lamp	(Page 25)
	Bring up table lamp L *of settee*	
Cue 14	**George** switches on kitchen lights	(Page 26)
	Bring up kitchen lighting	
Cue 15	George switches on lounge lights	(Page 26)
	Bring up all lighting in lounge	

ACT II, SCENE 1. Early evening

To open: Effect of September sunset

Cue 16	**Louise:** ". . . suits you fine, doesn't it?"	(Page 35)
	Start slow fade to dusk	
Cue 17	**George** draws lounge curtains	(Page 37)
	Increase interior fade	

Cue 18	**George** switches on desk lamp	(Page 37)
	Bring up desk lamp	
Cue 19	**George** switches on drinks table lamp	(Page 37)
	Bring up lamp on drinks table	
Cue 20	**George** switches on kitchen lights	(Page 37)
	Bring up kitchen lights	
Cue 21	**George** switches on lounge lights	(Page 37)
	Bring up remaining fittings	

ACT II, SCENE 2. Morning

To open: Effect of bright sunshine

No cues

EFFECTS PLOT

ACT I

Cue 1	**George** goes to kettle *Kitchen timer rings*	(Page 1)
Cue 2	**George** moves to kitchen table *Telephone rings*	(Page 1)
Cue 3	**George:** "Oh dear." *Loud pop music from upstairs*	(Page 2)
Cue 4	**George:** "... kidneys, I mean ... " *Sound of argument between Davey and Louise*	(Page 2)
Cue 5	**George:** "... Mummy in Bournemouth." *Loud crash upstairs*	(Page 2)
Cue 6	**George:** "... they're coming through!" *Door slam*	(Page 2)
Cue 7	**George:** "... can't concentrate." *Doorbell rings*	(Page 2)
Cue 8	**Louise:** "... haunted look about you." *Telephone rings*	(Page 7)
Cue 9	**Louise:** "... I'm not going to." *Doorbell rings*	(Page 12)
Cue 10	**Louise:** "... in your bedroom." *Doorbell rings*	(Page 12)
Cue 11	**Louise** exits to bedroom *Doorbell rings*	(Page 12)
Cue 12	**George** turns on taps *Doorbell rings*	(Page 17)
Cue 13	**George:** "... it's cocoa." *Telephone rings*	(Page 19)
Cue 14	**George:** "Tuesday's bridge night." *Telephone rings*	(Page 20)
Cue 15	**George:** "Jolly good, jolly good." *Telephone rings*	(Page 30)

ACT II

Scene 1

Cue 16	**Louise** lights cigarette *Telephone rings*	(Page 31)
Cue 17	**George** puts on record *Perry Como record starts*	(Page 37)
Cue 18	**George** goes towards fruit bowl *Doorbell rings*	(Page 37)

Cue 19	**George** stops record	(Page 37)
	Perry Como off	
Cue 20	**George** restarts record	(Page 42)
	Restart Perry Como	
Cue 21	**George:** "Is that quiet enough?"	(Page 42)
	Fade volume of record slightly	
Cue 22	**Louise:** "Then don't say it."	(Page 43)
	Shouts and laughter from upstairs, followed by general party noises	
Cue 23	**Louise** stops record	(Page 43)
	Perry Como off	
Cue 24	**Louise:** "Here we go again."	(Page 43)
	Loud pop music from upstairs, and voices. Continue throughout scene, swelling and dwindling as front door opens and closes	
Cue 25	**Louise:** ". . . Perry Como's mother or something?"	(Page 44)
	Shouts and laughter from upstairs	
Cue 26	**Louise** exits	(Page 50)
	Shouts of welcome and laughter after a moment, from upstairs	
Cue 27	**George** smashes record	(Page 50)
	Baby cries	
Cue 28	**George** exits through bedroom door	(Page 50)
	Telephone rings	
Cue 29	**George** bends over cot	(Page 50)
	Baby stops crying	
Cue 30	As CURTAIN falls	(Page 50)
	Pop music swells, to cover scene drop	

SCENE 2

Cue 31	As CURTAIN rises	(Page 50)
	Pop music fades out	
Cue 32	**George:** ". . . my sponge bag."	(Page 53)
	Telephone rings	
Cue 33	**Louise:** ". . . two Christian names, does he?"	(Page 58)
	Telephone rings	
Cue 34	**Louise:** ". . . with your mouth full."	(Page 59)
	Music swells as CURTAIN falls